REVIEWS

"Reading *Who Let the Dogs Out* is like hanging with your bestie and sharing stories over a glass of wine. Jackie is all at once funny, authentic, and insightful and makes you feel like you can get through it too. This book is like a Divorced Woman's right of passage and it assures you that you will come out the other side, better for it!"

Paige Morrow Kimball,
Award-winning filmmaker, writer and actor

"I give it five stars and a tail wag. While reading Jackie's incredibly honest and relatable account of her post-divorce dating adventures, I kept thinking of Julia Louis-Dreyfus's celebrated podcast, *Wiser Than Me*. Jackie's advice is heartfelt, timeless, funny, frank and shot through with a warmth you wouldn't expect from someone who's been called the C word on Valentine's Day."

Tammy LaGorce,
***New York Times* Weddings reporter**

"I love the way Jackie wove her thoughts, fears, and sheer joy throughout her dating stories. A must-read for any divorced person!"

Alyssa Dineen,
Online Dating Coach and author of *The Art of Online Dating*

"Jackie Pilossoph has mastered the art of blending humor with heartache in *Who Let the Dogs Out?*. If you're diving back into the dating pool, this book offers a lifeline of humor and practical wisdom that you won't find anywhere else."

Susan Guthrie,
Leading Family Law Attorney and Host of
The Divorce & Beyond Podcast

"Jackie doesn't hold back in sharing the cringe-worthy details of her encounters with emotionally unavailable partners, as well as her own less than perfect moments along the way. With humble vulnerability, Jackie invites readers into her own romantic struggles and missteps as she worked to rediscover herself and understand what healthy relationships looked like."

Karen Covy,
Divorce Coach, Lawyer, Mediator, and
Author of *When Happily Ever After Ends:*
How to Survive Your Divorce Emotionally, Financially and Legally

"Pilossoph infuses her narrative with authenticity and supportive undertones, making the reader feel like they're chatting with a wise friend. The book is both engaging and empowering, perfect for anyone navigating the end of a marriage and seeking both guidance and a good laugh."

Katherine E. Miller,
Divorce Attorney and Founder of the Miller Law Group,
New York and Connecticut

"Told with the same open-hearted warmth and honesty I've come to know and love from Jackie's podcast, this book is like sitting down with your best girlfriend with a glass of wine or cup of coffee and spilling ALL the tea! I am going to start sending it to all of my female clients at the end of their cases!"

Christine Diorio, Divorce Attorney,
Wills & Estate Planning Attorney, Tampa Bay, FL

"Relatable, funny and vulnerable. Grab your glass of wine, curl up on your couch and get ready to laugh, cry and thoroughly enjoy yourself as you read through Jackie's stories."

Maci Chance, Realtor,
Certified Divorce Specialist, Live Laugh Denver, Denver, CO

WHO LET THE DOGS OUT?

WHO LET THE DOGS OUT?

An Empowering, Funny, and Inspiring Guide to Dating After Divorce

Jackie Pilossoph

Founder of Divorced Girl Smiling

Who Let the Dogs Out?: An Empowering, Funny, and Inspiring Guide to Dating After Divorce

Published by Divorced Girl Smiling
Chicago, Illinois, U.S.A.

PILOSSOPH, JACKIE, Author
WHO LET THE DOGS OUT?
JACKIE PILOSSOPH

Library of Congress Control Number: 2024912867

ISBN: 979-8-9910390-0-0, 979-8-9910390-2-4 (paperback)
ISBN: 979-8-9910390-1-7 (digital)

FAMILY & RELATIONSHIPS / Dating
FAMILY & RELATIONSHIPS / Divorce & Separation
FAMILY & RELATIONSHIPS / Life Stages / Mid-Life
FAMILY & RELATIONSHIPS / Love & Romance
SELF-HELP / Personal Growth / Self-Esteem

Interior & eBook Design: Amit Dey (amitdey2528@gmail.com)
Publishing Management: Susie Schaefer (finishthebookpublishing.com)

QUANTITY PURCHASES: Schools, companies, professional groups, clubs, and other organizations may qualify for special terms when ordering quantities of this title. For information, email Jackie@DivorcedGirlSmiling.com

This book is dedicated to the Divorced Girl Smiling community—both those facing divorce and my Divorced Girl Smiling trusted professionals committed to serving them. You are courageous and beautiful, and you inspire me and my mission every day.

"The most exciting, challenging, and significant relationship
of all is the one you have with yourself. And if you find
someone to love you, well, that's just fabulous."
– **Carrie Bradshaw**

"One woman's trash is another woman's treasure."
– **Charlotte York**

"The good ones screw you, the bad ones screw you,
and the rest don't know how to screw you."
– **Samantha Jones**

"Do any of you have a completely unremarkable friend
or maybe a houseplant I could go to dinner
with on Saturday night?"
– **Miranda Hobbes**

AUTHOR'S NOTE

Readers should know that names (besides mine) and identifying characteristics have been changed, and, in some instances, characters were composited, locations and details recast, timelines altered, dialogue recreated from memory, and everything largely embellished to bring a little much-needed laughter to what can be a truly difficult time. The lessons I learned from these experiences are all very real and the advice I share is genuine. In regards to the advice presented in this book, it is solely for informational and educational purposes in the areas of divorce and dating. The book is meant to serve as a tool for self-help for personal use at your own discretion in conjunction with professionals that include: physicians, therapists, accountants, financial advisors, lawyers, mediators, and other professionals.

TABLE OF CONTENTS

INTRODUCTION

Fifty percent of all women will get divorced in their lifetime. Although divorce is devastating and scary and hurts like you wouldn't believe, with a good lawyer, a therapist and/or divorce coach, love of self, the ability to play pickleball, and of course, filler, most women end up pretty happy in their post-divorce lives. It's their ex-husbands who I worry about; their rowdy and sometimes inappropriate behavior—hence my comparing them to dogs in this book. Don't get me wrong, most of the men I dated after divorce were really good people deep down, but boy did so many of them behave like dogs (no offense. I don't want to insult actual dogs, just making a point).

I wrote this book for a few reasons. First and foremost, I cannot even count the number of tears I shed over the men (and one woman) I dated after my divorce, and why should all those tears go to waste? Something good should come from them. So, I decided to impart my hard-won advice by telling the stories—the outrageous, funny, heartfelt, tragic and very real stories (although some largely embellished) that I hope will help you if you are dating after divorce, whether it's only been a couple years or if it's your first time back in the game after twenty or thirty years.

Another goal of this book is to entertain you and make you laugh. So many women have told me how terrified they are of dating after divorce, of taking their clothes off with someone new, or even of kissing someone. Their fears come from not having dated in such a long time, feeling vulnerable, being afraid to trust someone again, not having self-confidence in their physical appearance, and having other insecurities. In my opinion, making light of something takes the fear out of it and makes it seem doable and manageable. Trust me, the guy who never called you back after your first date isn't going to be your biggest life problem, even though it may seem like it at the time.

Lastly, I didn't realize it back then, but in my dating after divorce adventures, I learned more about myself than I ever expected. I learned who I was, what I wanted and needed, and what I didn't want and need. My hope is that through my stories, the lessons I share, and my lists of tips and practical advice, you are able to apply this book to your dating life and:

1. See red flags.
2. Avoid many of the mistakes I made.
3. Not settle for bad behavior or any behavior that doesn't feel right to you.
4. Get out of toxic situations sooner than later.
5. Appreciate people for who they are and not try to change them.
6. Recognize the good ones.
7. Look deep within and be honest about what makes you happy.
8. Recognize the power of independence, whether you are in a relationship or not.

Let me be clear. I remember my dating after divorce journey in a very positive way. Despite the guys who made me cry, the ones who infuriated me, and those who made me feel like finding love was harder than accepting that Sex and the City was over, I have some really wonderful memories, some that I still think about today.

Who Let the Dogs Out is a book that comes from the bottom of my heart. It's honest and vulnerable, and meant to be funny—not spiteful. It's meant to inspire you that love after divorce, although not always easy to find, can be the best love yet. You just might have to date and put up with a few dogs before you find that perfect person, which begs the question, "Who let the dogs out?" Let me answer that for you. Who let the dogs out? All the women who divorced their husbands. They unleashed a group of men whose bark is loud, whose tail wags just a little too often, whose water bowl can be found at many local bars, and who might just follow you home. And, one of their dogs just might turn out to be the love of your life.

CHAPTER 1

The Lhasa Apso
(My Ex-husband)

The Lhasa Apso is beautiful on the outside. This breed is confident and playful, but tends to be a bit stubborn, at times. This trait really shined during our divorce.

This chapter is the only chapter in the book that takes place before my marriage and before my dating after divorce adventures began.

It was the summer of 1998, and at 32 years old, I was working as a TV reporter in Minnesota. I really felt like I was living my dream, but at the same time I was experiencing somewhat of a nightmare. I loved the job—reporting, writing, broadcasting, it was exciting and fun, and every day was an adventure. The problem was my boss, Henry, a cantankerous man who pretended to be cheerful all the time, when in reality he was only happy berating others while holding a gin and tonic in his hand. Henry also wanted to date me. When I politely declined (because he was married and old), he decided to make my life very difficult. How?

By sending me on the news stories no one else wanted, for example to a remote farm at 10:00 p.m. at night in a snowstorm to cover a horse manure spill. "Turn left after you see the second yellow house," was part of the directions I received. I had to drive alone, as the camera crew took a separate truck to set up. Remember, there were no cell phones back then, not that I'd have had reception anyhow. It was scary, freezing cold and smelly. Henry also held me back on an anchor job I was up for, telling the hiring manager, "She isn't ready yet." He constantly belittled and criticized me, making fun of my voice, my eyebrows, and my religion, to name a few things. I could never remember having such low self-esteem when I was around Henry, which was ironic because after a job search that had lasted almost two years, Henry was the one and only news director in the United States who took a chance on me and gave me a job. One weekend, I decided to drive to Chicago, where I had lived for several years prior, to visit my friends. I needed a break.

It was Saturday night, and I was out in the city with a few of my girlfriends. After a couple drinks, I decided to call my old boyfriend, Hudson. I'm going to compare Hudson to an American Pitbull Terrier because they are known for being tenacious and determined. Hudson had broken my heart by breaking up with me and getting back together with his ex-girlfriend, not once, not twice, but three times. Like the dog breed, he was determined to make it work with her, and every time the relationship failed, my phone would ring.

Leaving Hudson and Chicago behind, I had moved to Minnesota 10 months earlier, the combination of a weepy, brokenhearted girl and a motivated, career-driven woman. Now, here I was back in town visiting, and I had this intense curiosity to see Hudson, who was now broken up (again) with his girlfriend. Big surprise there.

Hudson was delighted to hear from me, and I ended up going over to his house that night. We talked for hours before I fell asleep in his arms. The next morning, Hudson told me he was seeing someone new, which reopened all the wounds from the past. Again, Hudson was putting me last. Things with him would never change. He just didn't love me. Period. Those were my thoughts on Sunday morning as I was walking up Clark Street to meet my friends at the Cubs game. I remember talking to God on the walk and asking, "What am I doing wrong? Why are all my friends getting married and I'm still as single as ever? Why doesn't Hudson love me? What's wrong with me? What have I done to deserve this loneliness? Will I ever have kids?"

Four innings into the game, I started to feel kind of nauseous. Keep in mind it was a sunny, very humid 95-degree day, I was dehydrated from the cocktails I'd had the night before, I was sleep deprived, and I was sitting in the extremely packed bleachers with my friend, her boyfriend, and a friend of his, who looking back was invited there as a set up. Although he was a really cute guy, my mind was still on Hudson. I suddenly felt claustrophobic and needed to get up and get some air. I made my way to the concession stand, purchased a bottled water, and stood there drinking it on the ramp that winds around on the outside of the ballpark. There was a nice breeze, and several people were doing the same thing.

All of a sudden, I noticed Charlie, the most beautiful person I had ever seen. Seriously. He was tall and had green eyes and dark hair. He looked like a J. Crew model who should be sitting on a sailboat looking out over the ocean, wearing nothing but seersucker swim shorts. He was standing a few feet away, looking at me and smiling, and I didn't really understand why. This might sound dramatic, but at that moment, time stood still, and I had the strangest feeling I've ever had in my life, a premonition that I was going to have kids with this gorgeous stranger. I can't explain it, I just knew it.

Charlie approached me and we started talking. As we were engaged in small talk (What do you do? Where do you live? Where are you from?), my head was swirling, and I began wondering if God had just answered my questions and prayers from earlier in the day. Charlie asked me what I was doing after the game, and I told him my friends and I were going to Murphy's (a bar in Wrigleyville, just outside the stadium) and that he should

3

meet us there. Then I said goodbye and headed back to the bleachers to tell my friends we had to go to Murphy's after the game.

When we walked into the bar, there was Charlie with another guy, who I assumed was his friend. We talked for a while and then Charlie asked if I wanted to go see a new movie called, *There's Something about Mary*, with him and a few of his friends. I told him I had plans that night, but that I wasn't leaving for two more days. Charlie and I went out for pizza the next night. At the end of the date, we kissed good night, and I asked him if he wanted to come visit me in Minnesota. I never thought about Hudson again. Suddenly, a man I'd been crazy about for months was magically erased from my mind. That's how much I liked Charlie, who came to Minnesota the next weekend.

Hosting someone from out of town who you barely know is pretty risky. Charlie was visiting me for an entire weekend, two nights and two full days. What if we didn't hit it off? What if it was awkward? What if he turned out to be a psycho? On the contrary, from the minute I answered the door, it was easy. We were acting like a couple already. We went out for dinner at a Mexican restaurant the first night, and the next day I took Charlie to a lake, where we went kayaking. It was very remote and extremely romantic, and we ended up swimming and kissing in the lake for a long time.

It was intimidating that Charlie was so good looking, but it was like he didn't even know it. He was a small-town guy, who was just really nice. He also made me feel safe. He had a good job where he was climbing up the corporate ladder. Charlie also had a great sense of humor. He made me laugh a lot, and to this day, I still think he is hilarious. Perhaps Charlie's biggest draw was that he seemed to be all in. He made me feel worthy of love and commitment. The way he looked at me, I felt like he loved me and at that time, that was something I desperately needed. He took the self-esteem I had lost from both Hudson and Henry and put it back in its place.

On the way home from the kayaking trip, we bought some corn from a guy selling it on the side of the road, and Charlie made a joke about how easily adaptable he was, meaning if his job didn't work out, selling corn might be a good alternative. He was funny and cute—not necessarily the most important traits to look for in a marriage, but it worked for now. The next day, we worked out at my gym and went to the outdoor pool there. That night, we went to a steakhouse and ate on the outdoor patio. It was very romantic, but the evening was cut short when we both started getting massively bit by mosquitos. By the end of the meal, we were wolfing down our food to get the check and get out of there. It was a story we would laugh about for years. When it was time for Charlie to go back to Chicago, we both felt sick. This was going to be really hard. I had never dated anyone long distance before, and I already felt very attached.

"How about if I stay another night?" Charlie asked.

"I'd love it!"

I made dinner for us that night, (which included the corn we bought) and Charlie and I made love. When he left the next morning, I was in love. God had given me what I had asked for while walking down Clark Street a week earlier. Nothing was clearer. The next day, a dozen red roses were delivered to me in my office, compliments of Charlie. My boss made a sarcastic comment and I wanted to punch him in the face.

For the next two weekends, I met Charlie at the University of Wisconsin, which was located in between where each of us lived. We agreed to pretend we were both professors at the University, just for fun. The weekends consisted of swimming, tanning, going out for romantic dinners, and of course, great sex. Those times were heavenly, and the first time we said "I love you" to each other is still something I'll never forget. A week or so later, Henry fired me. Please don't ask me why I didn't file a sexual harassment lawsuit. To this day, I regret it. He had no basis to let me go. In fact, there was no prior documentation of anything I'd done wrong. This was personal. Henry was jealous of my happiness and wanted me gone. When I look back at that whole situation, I think that Henry had crushed my self-esteem so deeply, that I left without even so much as a fight. It was like I was relieved to get away from the toxicity. I was tired. The bully had broken me. But I had Charlie.

I called him immediately. When he picked up his phone, while out to lunch with his 90-year-old grandmother, I started bawling.

"I just got fired," I managed to say through tears.

"That f*cker," Charlie said. "Well, you hate it there anyway. Move back here and live with me."

There it was. The fairytale, the prince rescuing me. I was ecstatic. Buh-bye, Henry, I'm out of here. Within a week, I sublet my apartment, hired movers, packed up my stuff, and get this: I had scheduled an interview with a pharmaceutical company. I would end up getting the job within two weeks after moving back, with a salary that was eight times what I was making at the TV station. It was like everything was meant to be. I was on this express train to wife and mother. 'Screw my career as a reporter,' I thought. 'All I got out of it was a boss who made my life miserable and made me feel badly about myself 24/7.' I was now 33 years old, and the clock was ticking. I was very happy to be starting my new life (again) back in Chicago, but this time with a man who loved me, a great job, and the promise of finally getting what I'd always wanted: a husband and babies. All that said, I'm not going to lie. Inside me was an ache buried deep within my heart because I knew what I was giving up—a promising journalism career. I loved writing and broadcasting. I really did (and still do, obviously). I want to add that in the midst of moving, I was offered an anchor job in Dallas, Texas. That's right. Dallas, the number five market for television news. I turned it down. It is a decision I still have a hard time reconciling today.

A year later, very comfortable in my high-paying career, Charlie and I got engaged. Eight months later we got married, and 14 months after that, I had my first child. As a whole, I remember these years as being really nice. On a side note, guess who ended up living a couple blocks away from us? Hudson and his new wife! I would run into him walking his dog in front of our building and I always got a kick out of Charlie getting jealous. Turns out, Hudson got married the same day as me. He did not marry the woman for whom he broke up with me three times. Another coincidence, Hudson and his wife had their first child within a couple weeks of us. Another twist: Hudson ended up working with and investing with a group of really smart businesspeople and became a multi-millionaire. When I dated him, he had no money. When I found out about his wealth 10 years later, it was a big ouchie for me, like twisting the knife just a little bit more to make the pain of him not loving me more intense.

Back to my marriage. Things were going pretty well, but there were some real underlying issues that I pushed aside and ignored. The first big thing that happened was my miscarriage. I had gotten pregnant right after our wedding and at thirteen weeks, I lost my first child. It was devastating. What was almost worse was the way Charlie handled the loss. I cried. He drank. I slept a lot. He became mean. I tried to talk to him. He turned it into an argument. But instead of addressing the issues, I covered them up by getting pregnant again. This time, I had a healthy baby boy, with whom I was madly in love (and still am.) The marriage was good again because things were good. When it's easy and everyone is happy, you just kind of keep moving along. But over the next few months and years, I was discovering that my husband and I were so unbelievably different. Now that we were parents, the fact that we had come from very, very different backgrounds and upbringings was becoming more and more of an issue. The differences in our childhoods were showing up in our parenting styles and the disparity between our approaches was causing tension, resentment, and loss of respect.

The intense and frequent fighting began right around the time I was pregnant with our second child. Our arguments were becoming more and more frequent, and I found that the times we were in a fight were far outnumbering the times we weren't. Our relationship wasn't good anymore. It wasn't meaningful and it wasn't fulfilling. It was becoming toxic and negative. We didn't know how to communicate, we didn't talk to each other with respect, we became mean to each other, and we didn't like each other. I also didn't like who I was with him. It seemed he brought out the worst in me. We weren't friends, we weren't a team, and we weren't thoughtful to each other. It was like the love was gone and we didn't know how to get it back. Where was that man I fell madly in love with while sitting in a kayak?

I'm not going to blame either of us for the demise of our marriage. We both contributed to its failure. I can only speak for my part, which was that I had run out of a toxic situation to let Charlie rescue me. In my wake, I had left behind a passion I worked so hard for, for such a long time. Money meant nothing to me. I'd have traded in my high-paying job in a minute to go back to news reporting. I think I was frustrated and bitter and resentful at both Henry and Hudson, so I was unhappy. As for Charlie's part in its failure, he was moody, hard to talk to, and had so many issues of his own that he hadn't dealt with. He had an angry side and took a lot of his unhappiness out on me. We tried marriage therapy, we tried individual therapy, and we tried romantic trips together. None of these things were effective enough to save it. We were both too far gone. At age 41, I now knew I had rushed into the relationship and had used it as a convenient escape from another bad situation. It was a pattern I'd developed, though it would take me years (and a great therapist) to realize that. At this point, it was time to file for divorce, and that is when I seriously entered hell.

Divorce, especially when your children are 3 and 5 years old, is so completely devastating, it almost takes your breath away. It's very sad, it makes you feel like a failure, it's a roller coaster of emotions, it's scary, it's confusing, it's infuriating, and it's depressing. It's like you're at war with your spouse, and like you are on trial when it comes to being a parent. If you screw up even once while in divorce litigation, your ex could deem you an unfit parent and you could lose custody of your kids. For example, when I was first getting divorced, I was drinking a lot to numb my pain. I'm not a big drinker, as a rule. One night, I was at a bar with a girlfriend, and I had had a few drinks. I planned on having dinner and not drinking anymore, so I would have been fine to drive home a couple hours later (which I realize now is not acceptable.) But I got a call from my babysitter that my then 4-year-old daughter had just thrown up. So, I darted out of the bar and made a U-turn to get home as quickly as possible. When I saw the flashing lights behind me, I almost died.

"Have you been drinking?" asked the cop who had just pulled me over.

I answered as if I was on autopilot, "Look, I just got a call from my babysitter. My 4-year-old daughter just threw up and I really have to get home to her."

Thank God, the cop let me off. I'm not sure if I'd have passed a breath-alyzer test, but had I been given one and failed, my divorce would have been a million times harder. My husband was so angry with me at the time, he would surely have tried to use it against me in court, and he probably would have been successful. From that day on and to this day, I have never had more than one drink and driven. That night was a warning sign from God, and the gift of a second chance. I have never taken that for granted.

Then there was the silent treatment. For about 9 years after our divorce, my ex-husband and his entire family did not speak to me. Seriously. Charlie even got remarried and his wife (now ex-wife) didn't speak to me either. Through all of our kids' activities, through their basketball, football and soccer games, and even at their Bar and Bat Mitzvahs, my ex and his entire family would not ever say hello to me. They were warm and embracing to my family but wouldn't give me the time of day! Do you know how that feels, especially when you're footing the bill for the entire party? It's incred-ibly sad and lonely, not to mention infuriating and frustrating. Then, about nine years after the divorce, Charlie started being nice to me. It was a little confusing, but I liked it. I also knew that he was not happy in his second marriage, and I think that played a big role. He and his family needed a vil-lain, and his new wife was now taking that on and letting me off the hook.

A few weeks after his attitude towards me changed, I asked him, "Why are you being so nice to me lately?"

He answered, "I decided I'm not mad anymore."

It's pretty insane that it took him 9 years for his divorce anger to go away.

Since then, we have become friendly, depending on the day, and how much money is involved in the conversation. After all these years, money still remains our biggest source of conflict. We do have our moments of kindness, but there are times when my resentment is as fresh as it was the day we decided to get divorced. I certainly have my issues in regard to the way my ex treated me during our marriage, in divorce, and after. But what I've come to realize is, you can still be friends with an ex despite that person's faults and behaviors. In other words, you can like parts of that person. Friendship with an ex doesn't even require respect for him or her. It's about tolerating more than you would from any other friend because you share children, and it's about that sentimentality that makes an ex feel like family. I'm not comparing my ex to my beloved family, but rather a cousin I care about. An ex isn't blood, but it's pretty darn close.

There have been highlights of a friendship with my ex that felt really nice, and sadly, I've come to realize those times were when my ex was unhappily married to his second wife, and right after he got divorced again. I sometimes feel a little bit like the friend he uses when he's lonely. Then again, when he got divorced, who was there trying to comfort him? Me. Despite everything with us, I felt sorry for him. At the beginning of Covid, when no one was leaving their homes, Charlie would come over and bring breakfast or lunch for the kids (who were in high school at the time), and he would sit and eat with them. Sometimes I would join them, and we would reminisce and laugh and tell the kids stories about our past together. The kids were beaming—thoroughly entertained and delighted to see their parents in this light. But I have to admit, it was fun for me too, to recall stories from such a happy time in life, especially in the midst of a pandemic that was really dark and scary.

I don't regret my relationship with Charlie. I don't regret marrying him and I also don't regret getting divorced. Our problems were impossible to work out, and had we stayed in the marriage all these years, I think it would have destroyed our kids. Children of divorce can still grow up to be happy, emotionally healthy, well-adjusted adults. A lot of how they end up depends on their parent's relationship in divorce. In my opinion, it's never too late for a couple to turn that around. If both parents are willing to put aside their personal feelings, as hard as that might be, and instead focus on being amicable, respectful, and kind to each other, their kids will feel it and reap the benefits. They will take that family stability with them and keep it in their hearts, just like kids who came from non-divorced parents. They have a better chance of growing up stable and secure, and therefore stronger and more self-confident. Those who watched their parents at war carry for the rest of their lives a fragile, precarious past, a result of their divided parents. I always hated the term, "broken home," because I think there are broken homes even when parents stay together. There are also healthy, happy homes in which parents got divorced. What's beautiful is that if you get divorced, you have full control over how you are going to parent and co-parent. You don't have control over how your ex is going to act and that can be difficult to manage, but if you focus on the choices you make, how you treat others, and how you parent, not only are you doing everything you can do, but you will live a happy life after divorce.

I bet there are many divorced people who regret marrying their ex-spouse. But I bet if you asked every single divorced person in the world if they regret having the children they had with their ex, they would all say, "no way!" Having kids is hands down, 100% the best thing I ever did and raising them is what I am most proud of in my life. My two children are the people I enjoy most in life. So, even though my marriage didn't work out, and even though the end of it was really painful, and even though going through a divorce was the hardest, most depressing time of my life, I wouldn't trade the past for anything. My two kids were born because I crossed paths with my ex. How could I possibly regret that?

The Emotional Stages of Divorce

Here are what I think are the emotional stages of divorce. At least, here's how they felt for me. I believe the stages are unique and occur in a different order for everyone, since every situation is unique. Also, there is no set period of time each stage can last.

1. Shock/disbelief/denial

This is when I just couldn't believe I was getting a divorce. It felt surreal. I kept trying to convince myself that maybe we could work things out. People call this bargaining. "I can live with the abuse…I can handle the fighting. It's not that bad. I will make it work. I just want him back." Sound familiar? It's like you're so scared of the unknown and of change, that you are rationalizing how you can make things work.

2. Sadness

In this stage, I felt the sadness of both breaking up with Charlie and realizing that we wouldn't be one of those couples who grows old together. My kids would now have divorced parents, and I wasn't going to have that happily ever after I thought I'd have. I was grieving my relationship and the future I always dreamed about.

3. Panic/fear/anxiety

How am I going to pay these attorneys bills? Do I have to get a job? Do I get to keep my house? Are my kids going to act out and cope in unhealthy ways? Am I going to be alone forever? Who's going to take care of me when I get sick? I don't even know how to pay a bill online. I don't understand finances or investing. I'm old. Who is going to want to date me? These are just a few of the million concerns that went through my mind at this stage. Everything was changing and it was really overwhelming and complicated and scary.

4. Anger/resentment

Now reality set in, and I was immensely angry with my ex. How could he do this to me? He took all my good years. He took advantage of me. He seems happy. I hate his guts. He treated me like crap all these years when I could have been with someone else. I resented everything about him and our past. I was also angry with myself, angry with God, and angry with anyone who did anything to remotely piss me off. Those poor customer service people who work for utility companies. I was so mean to them on phone calls, and I feel terrible about it.

5. A tinge of excitement/hope

During each of the stages there were little patches of hope, happiness, and excitement that kept me going strong and helped me to cope with the divorce, but during this stage, there was a lot of good stuff. I met a cute guy and realized I was still attractive to men. I became friends with a woman who was also going through a divorce. I started writing my first novel and was so proud of it. I saw a mouse in the house and learned how to take care of it. I became really proud of myself and all of my accomplishments and started to realize just how self-sufficient and independent I was. The future was suddenly looking promising. I was still frightened, but more optimistic than I'd ever expected.

6. Frustration

The divorce was taking forever to be final. One thing I learned is that it's smart to manage your divorce. What I mean by that is, you have to check in with your attorney and keep tabs on the case to make sure it's moving forward. That's not because the attorney isn't good at his or her job, and I'm not saying you should call your attorney every day, but I found that calling to "check-in" and ask where we were in the divorce, would spark movement. And movement is good in a divorce because it means the process will end sooner, which means less money and less stress. Another source of frustration was watching my ex with someone else. My ex was now dating my neighbor, and they seemed blissful. I'm sure she was seeing his best behavior and vice versa. Looking back, I think he wanted me to think they were really happy, and it worked. I was alone, and I'd see them together and I burned with anger. It didn't seem fair. Why does he get a happy ending and I am still miserable? I also felt like everyone in our community who saw them together probably thought I was the problem, and that since he was in this cute, blended family, he was the normal one. How wrong they were. My ex and my neighbor lasted less than 6 months.

7. Gratitude

As time went by, I started to realize that life was getting better, and I was thankful for that. The days of crying every hour were gone, and the days of crying every other hour were gone. I still cried. Don't get me wrong. But it was a lot less, with more joy and laughter and other good emotions starting to come back and occupy more of my daily life. I was grateful for the many people who had truly stepped up for me during this really hard time. I was more grateful for my family than I'd ever been. This was the time I started my gratitude practice, which is whenever you are feeling like you have a huge problem, shift your thoughts from worry and anxiety to the things that are going right and things that are working. To this day, I practice gratitude every morning. It's not always easy, but it works.

8. Acceptance

Total acceptance took years, but I had to reach a minimum level of acceptance before I could find a good life. My anger faded and I decided to take the attitude that everything was supposed to unfold this way. I accepted that I was now in my forties and single with two young kids. I accepted how I was wronged in the marriage and in the divorce. I accepted my financial situation. I accepted that my ex wasn't speaking to me. I find acceptance very empowering. Accepting is like saying, "I don't have control over this, so I'm going to focus on what I can control today and moving forward." Things weren't perfect (they never will be) but they were going in the right direction—better and better. When you accept, you are letting go so much anxiety and you feel so much less tired. It's a great feeling.

9. Empowerment

One day, several months into the divorce, I had had a really good day. That night, I looked in the mirror and realized I was so happy with myself for a lot of things. No one is perfect, but I was doing the best I could, given the circumstances, and I wasn't sitting around playing the victim anymore. I was tackling my problems, trying to be the best parent I could, and living life independently. I felt very grown up and there was a certain grace in that feeling. It was then that I started to feel strong and motivated to do more professionally. I got a job writing a column in a local newspaper for $50 a week. The first time I saw my name in the paper as the author, I was smiling from ear to ear. I never thought $50 would make me so happy, but it did because I was really proud of myself, and I knew that I was in the door at the paper. That little job would be the start of my print journalism career, and of Divorced Girl Smiling.

10. Peace

The stages of gratitude, acceptance, and empowerment culminated in a sense of peace. The kids and I were doing fine. Peace is just what it sounds like: quiet and serene, and maybe even a little boring, but in a good way. You don't think of your ex-husband and burn with anger. You think of your ex-husband and think, 'The past is in the past. I'm glad all that drama is behind me.' The feeling of peace is the feeling you get drinking a glass of wine overlooking a beautiful sunset, only you don't need the alcohol. Also, when you're at peace, that is when love and romance walk into your life unexpectedly.

Like the book so far? You'll love the podcast!

CHAPTER 2

The Bichon Frisé
(The One-Night Stand Guy)

The Bichon Frisé is outgoing, cheerful, and fun loving. This dog also loves to be the center of attention, which clearly, this guy was.

I want to share something with you that you might or might not know. A lot of newly separated women are f*cked up. Period. It's a fact. I include myself in this demographic. Our emotions are all over the place, and there are two things that are now our best friends: sex and passion. Sex and passion are fabulous substitutes for loneliness and fear. In other words, tonguing it in a bar with a stranger and telling yourself it's a miracle that you just met the sexiest, greatest guy on Earth is a very effective way to help you momentarily forget about all of your newfound sources of stress, such as finances, issues with your kids, and in-laws who now hate you, to name a few.

Another emotion strongly felt by the newly separated is sadness. We're mourning the loss of a partner, the end of a relationship, and the failure of a marriage. Then there's anger. We are pissed at our ex, at the world, and even at God. "Why did God do this to me?" We are also pissed at ourselves because deep down we know God didn't do it to us, we did it to ourselves. "Why did I marry the wrong guy?" "Am I a horrible person who deserves all this pain?" "How could I have been so stupid marrying this guy?" There is also a feeling of desperation: "Who is going to want me now that I'm old?"

These are some of the emotions swirling around and the rational and irrational questions we are asking ourselves that contribute to our mindset of panic and confusion and behavior that isn't typical of who we really are. We're just not ourselves. The good news is this mindset is usually only temporary. In time, we become ourselves again, and even better versions of ourselves if we do the work to heal emotionally. When it comes to the newly separated, we could be totally fine one minute, and the next find ourselves screaming and giving the finger to a slow driver. Anxiety is off the charts, highs and lows are extreme (with more lows), and fear is almost unbearable. But there is something else we're carrying, a guilty secret that feels shameful to share for fear of being judged. What is it? A tinge of joy and excitement for the future, for a better life, and yes, for the possibility of finding love again. But that's down the road. A newly separated women doesn't want to be in love at this moment. What we want in the early days of a divorce is sex and passion.

When my ex-husband moved out of our house in the summer of 2007, I had mixed emotions about living alone with my two toddlers. On one hand, I felt immense relief that there was no more walking on eggshells and trying to fix something that had no chance of working. In many ways, limbo is a lot worse than when you come to the realization that the divorce is actually going to happen. The house is peaceful but it's also quiet and lonely. Despite the sense of relief, the feeling of emptiness is all around. Living with two toddlers might give others the impression that you don't feel isolated because you are busy and not ever alone. I actually think living as a single mom with young children makes a person feel even more isolated, not because we don't love and appreciate the kids, but because they are so little that you have to protect them by hiding your feelings every minute. There's this immense pressure to make sure they don't see you cry, become angry and enraged, or say anything negative—the three things you want to do on an hourly basis! It's actually a very lonely and frustrating feeling.

Then there's the way you feel about yourself physically. I remember losing weight without even trying, but wearing sweatpants every day so I wasn't even noticing. I would rarely wear makeup because I cried so much; I didn't see the point of mascara running down my cheeks. Towards the end of my marriage and for the first several months after we started divorce proceedings, I felt frumpy, old, and undesirable. Until one night, when a chance encounter would make me feel like a lion who was just let out of her cage.

It was New Year's Eve. Not surprisingly for Chicago, the weather that night was freezing cold and snowing like crazy, but that wasn't going to stop me. For some reason, I had a compulsion to go out. I didn't want to start the new year sitting home and crying, and my kids were spending the holiday with my ex, so I had an empty house. While doing fitness classes at my gym, I had met a woman named Susan who was also getting divorced. The two of us became instant best friends. Years later, I would look back and realize that it was a superficial friendship between two women who had nothing in common except for the fact that they were both going through a divorce, which is to say, they had everything in common. Susan and I had gone out for dinner a few times and had hit some bars together, talking and flirting harmlessly with divorced men on almost every occasion.

Susan picked me up, and because of the weather, we decided to stay close to home, choosing a sushi restaurant in my neighborhood. I will say, my intention was to go home right after dinner. While we were eating, I got a call from one of our girlfriends from the gym.

"Hey! Please come over to the wine bar. We'd love to see you. It's not that crowded here, I promise!"

The wine bar she was referring to was right across the street, so we paid the bill and headed over. It wasn't packed, but there was a nice crowd, and it had a good vibe. After a drink and a few hellos to some people who lived in my neighborhood (mostly couples and women from the gym), I looked at Susan, and asked, "Can we go? I'm tired."

"I'm so glad you said that. Let's go."

We headed for the door and that's when I saw this adorable guy sitting at the bar. He had a really cute look about him with his messy light brown hair and brown eyes. As we were walking by, he blatantly turned around and asked, "Are you guys leaving?"

I looked at Susan, who gave me a confused look.

All of a sudden, I perked up and transformed into a flirty party girl. "We were leaving, but now I think I want to stay."

Susan laughed.

The guy, who I estimated to be in his mid to late thirties, flirted right back. "I'm so happy to hear that."

"Should we get another drink?" Susan asked.

"I got this," said the guy, "What do you guys want?"

He ordered the drinks and then told us his name was Mike, that he lived in Los Angeles, and that he was in town visiting his family for Christmas. There with two of his high school buddies, Mike shared that he worked in computer consulting and happened to be a minister on the side for the sole purpose of marrying couples.

"I've never been married, but I love weddings, and I'm pretty spiritual," Mike said. "I've married like eight couples so far."

A shot glass appeared in front of me, courtesy of Mike. Susan had disappeared.

"You're the cutest minister I've ever seen," I said as if I had no control of what came out of my mouth. I then grabbed the shot glass and downed what turned out to be tequila.

"What do you do?" Mike asked me.

The question felt like a punch in the stomach. How was I supposed to answer? "I was a promising reporter at one point in my life, as well as a successful pharmaceutical sales representative, who made the stupid decision to become a stay-at-home mom five years earlier"?

I want to clarify that I have nothing against stay-at-home moms, and that I respect people who go that route because of all the jobs I've ever had, I think being a stay-at-home mom is the hardest. The thing was, staying home with the kids wasn't a good fit for me. Despite the fact that I absolutely adored my toddlers, I didn't enjoy spending my days playing with toys, cleaning up every minute, and dealing with temper tantrums. Being a stay-at-home mom can feel lonely and isolating. It's also very boring, at times. I remember I used to watch the clock because I couldn't wait for the day to end. How sad is that? Being a stay-at-home mom is also a thankless job, and very bad for self-esteem because you don't get paid, and you don't get recognized for anything you do. Add in an unhappy marriage, and for me, it was a disaster. Also, let's not forget that slice of regret creeping its way into my soul for letting my former bully boss lead me to give up a promising journalism career.

But what's even harder than being a stay-at-home mom is being a separated stay-at-home mom. I mean, if you're with the kids all day, where do you go to break down crying when your lawyer calls you and gives you bad news about your case? Where do you go when you feel like you need to scream your head off in anger about how your ex is acting? Where do you go when you feel so stressed you almost can't breathe? Nowhere. You put a fake smile on your face and continue playing Candy Land as your heart is slowly breaking.

"So, what do you do?" Mike asked again.

Suddenly, the answer came to me as clear as day. "I'm a writer."

This was not a lie. When I got separated, the flood gates opened, and I spent every free second of my life writing. For some reason, journaling my pain helped immensely. It was therapeutic and validating. Putting my feelings on paper (OK, on the computer screen) felt like someone was listening to me, understanding me, and helping me clarify how I felt.

"Cool, what do you write?"

"I'm working on a novel about a woman with two toddlers, who is going through a divorce."

"Based on a true story?" he nervously chuckled.

"Sadly, yes," I said.

"That's actually sexy."

"You're sexy," I replied. Then I burst out laughing. "Wait, did I just say that?"

Mike was laughing. Then he leaned in and kissed me. To say I enthusiastically participated is putting it mildly. A 41-year-old newly separated woman has more passion inside of her than a teenage boy, just FYI. More drinks, more flirting, and more kissing, continued. I looked around the bar for Susan and saw her socializing with Mike's buddies. Right then, I started thinking, 'No one's home, Mike's flying back to Cali in a few days, and I haven't had sex in almost a year. Hmmm….'

"Hey, I live walking distance from here," I said. "Want to come over?"

"Uh…sure," he said. "Are you sure?" He seemed shocked.

Looking back, this was a very stupid idea. Taking a complete stranger to your house in the middle of the night with no one home is asking for trouble. I knew nothing about Mike. He could have hurt me, raped me, killed me, stolen from me, you name it. But he didn't. Mike and I got home a few minutes before midnight. It was very romantic having a glass of wine, toasting, and kissing a complete stranger when the clock struck 12. It was about 12:01 when we decided to go up to my bedroom.

Clothes started coming off. The kissing was intense, and the passion was like none I'd ever experienced. Not knowing someone I was about to have sex with was completely new for me. I had never, ever done this. I sort of felt like I was in a romance novel. For the first time since I'd gotten separated, I felt like I was being given a gift; an experience I wouldn't have had if I wasn't going through a divorce. Being half naked in a man's arms made me feel feminine and young again, like life wasn't over and like romance was still a possibility for me. It was also about temporarily forgetting my problems and my fears. It was about not being lonely for the first time in ages. Just for tonight, I wanted to pretend that a man loved me. Unfortunately, I just couldn't.

All of a sudden, I started to feel suffocated. Everything felt wrong. I wasn't ready to have sex with a stranger. I wanted to run. I wanted to scream. I wanted out of this whole situation. What was I doing?! I was a wife and a mother, not some bar chick who takes guys home and screws them. So, I pushed Mike away from me and breathlessly managed to say, "Stop, please. I can't do this."

Mike backed off and asked if I was OK. With tears in my eyes, I took a deep breath and answered, "I'm so sorry. This was a mistake."

Then I hurriedly put my clothes back on and Mike did, too, and we walked downstairs. Mike asked me for my address. Then he texted someone, who I assumed was his ride home. We stood there in silence for a minute and then Mike asked, "Are you OK?"

"Yes," I managed. "I'm truly sorry for all this. I'm really messed up right now."

Mike looked at me and when he spoke, I realized what I good minister he was.

"It's OK. We're all a little messed up."

I smiled at him.

"Can I give you a hug?" he asked.

"Sure."

Shortly after, I heard a horn honk.

"That's my buddy," said Mike. Then he opened the door and turned back to me before he left. With a sad face he said, "Take care, Jackie. Happy New Year."

"Happy New Year, Mike."

The goodbye was sweet, but it was also awkward, and as soon as the door closed, I burst into tears. Who was I and what the hell had I just done with my life? What was I thinking getting divorced? Was it better to be unhappy in a marriage or be this person who just almost had sex with a stranger? What was going to happen to me? Were the choices: be alone and lonely or start dating? I didn't feel like I had the strength to date or sleep with people, but I also knew I didn't want to be alone. After all, I had gotten married because I wanted a family. That family fell apart and tonight had been a grim reminder. I felt bitter and angry and hopeless and depressed, and I cried myself to sleep.

I woke up the next morning with a guilt and self-hatred hangover, feelings that would last for several days. I hated myself for the way I'd behaved the night before, and for bringing a complete stranger home. What a stupid risk to take! God was truly watching out for me in that Mike turned out to be a nice guy. He was understanding. Who knows? Another guy might have been angry, insistent, and forced himself on me. I couldn't eat and I could barely focus on anything else but regret and shame. When my kids came home, I was so grateful to see them, and to be their mom. It was then that deep down I knew I needed help to deal not just with my post-divorce feelings, but to examine my life and my choices, which meant looking all the way back to childhood. Sadly, it would be a long time before I chose to seriously commit to therapy.

To this day, I have regrets about Mike. Someone who would have a one-night stand just isn't who I am, and even having come close to it, I felt guilt and shame. I don't judge other people who have had a one-night stand or stands, so why was I judging myself? Every person's story is unique, and so are the reasons for their choices. But I will warn you to be careful of bringing a stranger to your home or going to theirs. It is risky. I was lucky. Please, please think carefully and don't let alcohol cloud your judgement.

I would also tell anyone who is thinking of having a one-night stand that it might cause you to feel bad about yourself emotionally. I'm talking about low self-esteem, lack of self-love, the feeling of having been used, and the feeling you did something wrong (which is not the case). Try to remember that you deserve more than a one-night stand. I've heard a lot of women say things like, "If guys can have a one-night stand, then why can't I? Maybe that's what I want." I disagree. I think women want to feel empowered by having sex with a stranger that they will be just fine having a casual fling, but are then surprised at how disappointing, empty, and lonely it can leave them. I think women have a much harder time than men separating sex and emotions, but there are likely some men who have a hard time having casual sex. Especially divorced men. In the end, your body is yours and so is your choice of sexual partners. But there's nothing that beats sex with someone who you know cares about you and loves you. It's the best and it's worth the wait.

Safe sex is good sex.

Safe sex after divorce is just as important as safe sex was before you were married. And for those of us with children, it's actually more important because we now have them to think about. I can't believe the number of divorced men and women who tell me they have unprotected sex with people they either just met or with whom they have yet to have the sex history talk. They look at me with this innocent (I like to call it naïve and stupid) look and say, "Well…I'm sure it's fine."

My question is, how can you possibly know it's fine? You have no idea who that person has slept with. It baffles me how adult men and women can preach safe sex to their children and then disregard their own advice and have unprotected sex themselves. Look, I'm not trying to be judgmental, but it really scares me. You have a responsibility to yourself and your children to make sure you stay healthy and live a long life. I cannot understand how someone can take that risk. I just can't.

Safe sex is still fun.

What's the big deal about using a condom until you really get to know the person, until you know that person's history, and most importantly, until you know the two of you are exclusive? Doesn't that make sense?

How to have the sex history talk.

Here's where it might get tricky. Here's a scenario. You meet someone and the two of you are gaga over each other. It's only your second date, but you've had a couple glasses of wine, and you are absolutely loving this person. You might even think he or she is the one. After months (or even years) of being alone and feeling hopeless, like there is no one out there for you, you finally meet this person you really like. Plus, you are so physically attracted, and you've been lonely for so long, all you want to do is rip this person's clothes off. I totally understand that. But what I'm saying is that you have two choices: you either use a condom or you have the sex history talk. The sex history talk probably isn't going to happen during the heat of passion, let's be honest. So, I'd recommend the condom at that moment.

Have the sex history talk while you are both sober and not in bed. Maybe start off by saying, "I know this is awkward and not easy to talk about, but would you be okay with us talking about our sexual pasts?" Then the two of you need to be honest and upfront with each other. I've also known couples (including myself and my current partner) who were both tested for STDs before having unprotected sex. I support that idea 100% and think it's very wise.

In closing, sex after divorce can be wonderful. Enjoy yourself and your new love. You deserve those breathtakingly passionate moments. But remember that sex is also so powerful that it can cloud your judgment. I encourage you to be smart and responsible when it comes to sex. Being safe doesn't lessen the pleasure. In fact, knowing you're being safe will most likely make the sex even better!

CHAPTER 3

The German Shepherd: (The Hot and Cold Guy)

The German Shepherd is confident and smart, but can also be aloof (i.e. cold), especially to people who aren't family or close friends, which included me.

I didn't want to do it. I really didn't. But, my friend, Sheila kept nagging me. "Come on…Brad's single, you're single now…" It had been a few months since my ex moved out and I hadn't gone out on any dates yet unless you count Mike, which I wouldn't. I wasn't even close to being officially divorced yet, so I felt a little bit weird about dating and being seen with guys around my suburb. People talk, you know. Then again, I guess I wasn't feeling weird on New Year's Eve.

On a side note, I had no idea at the time that my ex had started dating our much younger than me neighbor—two weeks after he moved out! We had both met this woman, with her fake personality and fake boobs, at the bus stop with our kindergarteners. I didn't find out about them for months, months during which I could never understand why this bus stop bitch was so unfriendly and rude to me all the time! As you can see, I'm still traumatized by it. But back to the Brad story. I gave in to Sheila and agreed to meet her and her husband and Brad at a local bar.

Within the first half hour or so, I was pleasantly surprised that I was interested in Brad. I mean, isn't it sort of a given that the first date you have after your divorce is going to be a nightmare? Aren't you supposed to go home and cry and feel hopeless about ever finding love again? That wasn't the case with Brad. Brad was older, bald, and short, but he had some very attractive qualities. He was witty, charming, and had a quiet confidence about him that was appealing. Brad was a self-made wealthy man who was raising two young kids after his wife left the family and moved out of state. Just knowing that gave him my instant respect. I didn't know any single dads yet, let alone dads who were really single, meaning they were parenting all on their own. That made Brad kind of sexy.

If I had to guess, we were at the bar for about an hour when Sheila got a call from her babysitter saying that one of their kids was having a temper tantrum and wouldn't go to bed. So, they left pretty quickly, leaving Brad and me alone. I have to be honest, I was kind of happy about it. I liked Brad, and now this really felt like a date. After another drink, we decided to leave. Brad paid the bill and while we were walking to our cars, he asked if I wanted to continue the party at his house, which was a couple blocks away. Stupidly, I said yes.

We ended up walking to his house, which turned out to be a mansion. I was trying to hide my shock at how big and beautiful it was. This would be the first of many times in my post-divorce life that I saw wealth and wondered how the person made all that money, and where I had gone wrong in life when it came to finances. But I knew the answer to that question. I had chosen to give up a lucrative career in sales to become a stay-at-home mom, and let's not forget the journalism career. When I was single, and even when I was married, money wasn't very important to me. I didn't buy myself many material things, I didn't care what kind of car I drove, and I didn't take lavish vacations because I had little kids, and what fun is it to go to the Amalfi Coast or Santorini or St. Thomas with two toddlers? Money only became very important to me when I started going through a divorce and naively thought about how much easier having money could make things. Walking into Brad's house, I thought about his divorce, and how he probably didn't even think twice about paying his attorney fees or paying alimony. He was so financially secure. What I would learn later is that divorce is hard for everyone, no matter how much or how little money someone has, because the more money you have, the more there is to fight about in court, which results in higher attorney's fees and larger alimony checks. And, over the years, I met a lot of men (and women, actually) who had money and a lot of men and women who didn't have money and they all seemed to have something in common: they hated paying child support and alimony. It was the principle, not the money. Anger and resentment and bitterness made them not want to pay.

"Want another drink?" Brad asked me when we got to his kitchen—my dream kitchen.

"Where are your kids?" I asked.

"They're staying with my parents tonight."

Had Brad planned this out? Did he want to give himself the option of bringing me back to his place if the date went well? Those thoughts were offensive and flattering at the same time. So cocky. On the other hand, we were here, weren't we? Our first kiss was on his couch in front of the fireplace. Kissing a wealthy, divorced, older guy was sexy, but it also felt safe.

"You're really pretty," said Brad, in between kisses.

This was getting good. I started thinking that I could see Brad becoming my boyfriend. He was going to sweep me off my feet, rescue me, and life was going to be perfect! Then he said four words that completely wiped away that theory.

"Want to go upstairs?"

What?! My hopes suddenly came crashing down.

"No, I think I should go," I said. Then I stood up.

Brad laughed. "Wait a minute. Sorry if that freaked you out. I really like you. In fact, I'd love to go out again."

That was somewhat redeeming.

"OK, that sounds good," I said. "But I really do want to go home."

"Sure," he said. He walked me to my car, and I was pleasantly surprised when he held my hand on the way. We said good night and after one more kiss, I got into my car, drove home smiling, and went to bed feeling really wonderful.

The next day felt strange. Based on what a nice night we had had, I was expecting a phone call or a text from Brad. Nothing. Nothing the next day either or the next. A week went by and still nothing. It felt awfully cold. As a newly separated woman in my forties, I'd put my vulnerability on the table, only to feel exposed, hurt, and stupid. The rejection I felt from Brad was beyond awful. Was this a glimpse at how the post-divorce dating world worked? Was Brad a sample of the men in the pool of suburban divorcees?

I sort of gave up on Brad. I mean, what choice did I have? But then, a couple weeks later I ran into him at a bar. My heart started pounding the second I saw him. I was angry and wanted to say, "You're a jerk." But before I even said hello, Brad was turning on the charm and his smile, funny jokes, and lightheartedness made any negative thoughts about him vanish. He immediately ordered me a drink and after one more convinced me to go back to his place. Like an idiot, I did, but not before asking, "Hey, why didn't you ever call me after the first night we met?"

"Yeah...." he replied. His face turned sad, almost like a dog who realized you just saw the crap he took on the dining room rug. He continued, "I was sort of seeing someone, and it just ended, and that's kind of where my head has been."

My gut was screaming, "What a crock of shit," but it was easier and more convenient to accept this as an answer. Back at the mansion, we began kissing again, and just as he did the first night, he asked if I wanted to go upstairs. And just like the first night I declined. I started disliking myself right then. This was a complete repeat, and I knew it, especially the next couple days when I waited for texts or calls that would never come. For the next couple months, Brad became my hook-up guy—kissing only. I would text him if I was out or vice-versa and we would meet at one of our houses, have a drink, talk a little bit, and make out. I talked myself into the fact that this relationship was what I wanted.

"You don't want anything serious right now," "This is all you can handle." "This is the perfect relationship for you." "Why get hot and heavy with someone right now?" I rationalized Brad's treatment of me but deep down, I hated our relationship. I hated Brad for being hot and cold and playing games with my newly separated heart, but most of all, I hated myself for staying in it. I think Brad stayed in it hoping to get me into bed, which never happened. My therapist at the time told me that my obsession with trying to get the hot and cold guy to be hot only was squeezing out any room I had in my head when it came to mourning the end of my marriage. Convenient, isn't it? Think about it. Isn't it easier to focus on a small love life issue than all the problems that come with getting divorced at 41 with two young kids? My relationship with Brad eventually fizzled, and I was left feeling hurt, resentful, and disappointed, both in him and in me.

About a year later, I ran into Brad at a high-school football game. We waved and smiled at each other, and I really didn't think much of it. I had no expectations except that I wouldn't hear from him. So, wouldn't you know, the next day he called. I immediately sensed a different tone. After a few minutes of polite conversation, he shocked me by asking me if I wanted to come stay at his Vail, Colorado ski house with a group of people. He suggested I ask one of my girlfriends to come, and the two of us could share one of the nine bedrooms. I was elated. Maybe Brad had changed. Maybe I caught him at a bad time last year. Maybe now he was ready to go from hot and cold to just hot. I was very excited and happy.

A couple weeks later, my friend Susan and I flew to Vail to meet Brad and his houseful of friends. Not shockingly, his Colorado home was even larger than his other mansion. I was so excited to be there and very flattered I had been invited to such a beautiful place. Brad had to have liked me if he invited me here, right? Wrong. While the weather was picture perfect, clear skies, white, fluffy snow, and hot sun, Brad treated me as cold as the icicles that were hanging over the rooftops. He rarely spoke to me the entire trip, but there were tinges of interest. For example, he texted me while Susan and I were skiing, asking me to meet him for lunch on top of the mountain. But once we got there, he sat at the other end of the table of 12 and didn't say a word to me. The last night of the trip, Brad had a party at his house. I finally worked up the nerve to confront him.

"Why am I here?" I asked bluntly.

Brad responded with a nervous giggle, "I need another drink for that conversation."

"Seriously, I really want to know why you invited me since you haven't talked to me all weekend. What are we? Are we friends? Are we more?"

Brad's response was sort of vague and included the words "I'm going through a bad time," "I'm f*cked up," and "I really like you and think you're really pretty."

"So, what should we do?" I asked.

"I'm going to bed," he replied. "You know where I live."

Now my jaw was on the ground. What was I supposed to do? Given the way I'd been treated, I wasn't ready to sleep with Brad. But maybe if I went to his room we could talk more. So, a couple hours later, while everyone in the house was asleep, I tiptoed to his room. My heart was racing, and I was really scared. I couldn't handle any more hurt from Brad, but it was like I had to know what he was thinking. The suspense was almost killing me. I'd flown all this way and needed to know. I felt like my visit to Brad's room could turn out badly or it could be the turning point of our relationship. It was kind of exciting, in a way. I held my breath, turned the knob, and that's when I got a huge shock. His door was locked! Brad had invited me to his room and then locked his door on me. If that wasn't the epitome of hot and cold, I don't know what is. My heart sank. I felt played. I felt embarrassed. I felt like a fool.

The next day, which was the day we were leaving, I confronted Brad. I figured, why not? I'm never, ever going to speak to this complete dick ever again. "You know, I went to your room last night and the door was locked," I said. Hearing these words come out of my mouth made me realize right then that this guy did nothing for me except make me feel like a complete loser. I was so humiliated that to this day it's hard to write about. Brad's reaction? He started getting angry and telling me the door wasn't locked and that he wasn't feeling well that night. It was such an immature and dishonest response that it finally hit me: I needed to get the f*ck out of Colorado and as far away from Brad as I could.

As my plane was taking off, a few tears rolled down my cheeks and Susan patted my arm. They weren't tears of sadness but rather tears of burning anger. I was furious at Brad and his hot and cold treatment. How could someone treat another person that way, especially a person who was newly divorced? The truth was, I let him do it to me, and I was mad at myself for a pretty long time. I realized that Brad brought out someone in me who I didn't care for: a desperate person with barely any self-confidence. That person isn't who I am at all. It wasn't even who I was as a newly divorced person.

Here's what I failed to pick up on sooner while involved with Brad and the advice I want to offer: Someone who is acting hot and cold is messed up. Their behavior is not your fault, and it has nothing to do with you. It has everything to do with the hot and cold person. If a person treats you nicely one day and not-so-nicely the next, how can that possibly be a reflection on you? It isn't. It is all about the hot and cold person's issues of confusion, self-doubt, and unhappiness. Maybe the person has deep-seated anger for his ex and is somehow transferring those feelings to you. Maybe that's their personality, and they treat every romantic partner this way. Whatever the case, the treatment isn't because of something you did or didn't do or the person you are, and it's not your fault! The sooner you learn to place the hot and cold treatment on the person who's treating you that way, the sooner you will get out of the toxic relationship, like yourself more, and understand how unhealthy the hot and cold person really is. You might even feel sorry for him or her.

Know When It's Time to Walk Away

There's an old saying that goes, "If someone shows you who they are, they shouldn't have to show you again." I should have known from day one, the day after my first date with Brad when he didn't contact me, that he was wrong for me. Whether Brad was hot and cold by nature (to everyone), or it was bad timing, or it was just me to whom he chose to be hot and cold, how he treated me, whether he realized he was doing it or not, was very wrong. It was mean and toxic, and I wasted so much time worrying about it and trying to make a relationship work that didn't have a chance from the start.

I'm not saying that you should never give someone a second chance. People make mistakes and they deserve the benefit of the doubt and the opportunity to change. But if someone treats you a certain way that is undesirable to you over and over and over again, have the confidence and self-love to walk away. It's not always easy. Hope in a relationship stems from all the wonderful qualities you might see in someone or the person's potential that you imagine in your mind. These things may cause you to be patient, to keep trying to help your love interest be the person you want them to be, and to keep hoping they'll treat you differently—next time. But the key to finding a happy, healthy relationship is having the courage to face reality. How is this person treating you right now? You deserve better than hot and cold, even if it means ending the relationship and being alone for a little while. You deserve to be treated "hot" at all times. It's the key to self-love, trust and joy. In other words, hot is worth the wait.

CHAPTER 4

The Golden Retriever
(The Way Too Nice Guy)

The Golden Retriever is affectionate, gentle, and calm. This dog likes pleasing their owner. It's a shame his "owner," i.e me, was too stupid to appreciate him.

"Hindsight is 20/20," "everything looks clearer in the rearview mirror," and "if only you'd known then what you know now," are the phrases associated with the guy you call "the one who got away."

The one who got away is the guy who adored you, who treated you amazingly, and who would have done anything for you. He's the guy who was emotionally healthy, who came from a great family, and who wanted to be married. He's the same guy who you decided was just too into you, too clingy, and not exciting enough. The spark just wasn't there, and you felt suffocated.

He's also the same guy who years later you see on Facebook, who looks even better than when you dated him and who seems blissfully happy with his new wife. Oh, and he's the same person who you heard through the grapevine invested his money really well, now has a winter condo in

Florida, and is getting ready to retire at age 60. The one who got away is someone who makes you feel regret and who causes you to call yourself an idiot. Idiot Pilossoph's one who got away goes by the name of Noah.

I met Noah at a friend's out-of-town second wedding. He and I both went to Indiana University, but I didn't know him there. The people who were getting married were mutual friends of ours. The first thing I noticed about Noah when I saw him was his cute dimples and his athletic body. I think Noah might have played football at Indiana, despite the fact that he was 5'10." This was the first indication that he was driven, disciplined, and motivated to achieve anything he wanted.

I asked my friend who he was, and she got really excited.

"I thought you were dating that single dad," she said, referring to Brad.

I tried to keep the bitter tone out of my response. "Nope."

"Noah would be perfect for you!"

She told me Noah was newly divorced. Apparently, his wife had an affair with her personal trainer, left him, and was now engaged. If someone would have asked me why Noah was divorced, without ever having had a conversation with him, I could have told you that it wasn't his decision. He did not look like the kind of guy who would do something to jeopardize his marriage.

My friend introduced us, and I talked to Noah all night. He was warm and kind and easygoing, just one of those guys that everyone likes. He had a successful office supply wholesale business and beamed when talking about his three kids, who at the time were in grade school and middle school. Noah was the first glimpse of hope I had that there were nice, divorced guys out there. The problem was, I wasn't sure if I was ready for nice. I was so used to jerks that nice seemed a little foreign. I realize now how messed up that sounds.

That night, we exchanged numbers. Noah was living in Indianapolis, and I was in Chicago, so the only way we could get together was if one of us visited each other or if we met somewhere. Noah called me a couple days later and asked what I was doing the following weekend.

"My kids are with their dad, so I'm actually going home to visit my parents," I said.

"In Pittsburgh?" Noah asked.

"Yes."

"That's so funny," he said. "I'm actually going to be in Pittsburgh next weekend."

"Really?" I asked in a skeptical way.

"Yeah, my buddy lives in Pittsburgh."

I broke into a huge grin. "That's such a coincidence. What town?"

"Uh…. I forget."

An awkward silence followed, and then Noah added, "Look, I'm going to be there and would love to get together one night."

At that moment, I was beyond flattered. No man had ever made such an effort to see me. It made me feel special and important. It felt really great, but at the same time it was scary. This guy was going to drive seven hours, and in my heart, I knew it was all for me. In the end, I agreed because I felt like a nice guy might be just the refreshing change I needed. It felt like the first healthy romantic encounter since the divorce.

It wasn't a big surprise that the second I landed in Pittsburgh, Noah called me to ask what I was doing that night. I told him I didn't have any plans besides hanging with my parents, and he said he'd see me in about an hour. I then had to explain to my mom and dad that this guy I met at a wedding last weekend was coming here to take me out on a date. They were actually very happy about it, especially when I told them he drove here for me. They were over-the-top ecstatic when I told them his stats: wealthy, single dad whose wife left him.

The funniest part of the whole weekend was when Noah rang the doorbell, my dad answered the door to find him standing there with his suitcases. So now, Noah was staying with us! I still remember my dad trying so hard not to laugh. We showed Noah to the guest room, and shortly after that, we took my parents car, went to a bar, and had a really fun night. We danced and talked and laughed and told stories. It felt so comfortable, like I was with my best friend, who was also really cute. Noah kind of felt like family. What a fairytale this whole thing had turned out to be. At the end of the night, Noah kissed me and went to his room. It was sweet. I went to bed happy and excited. I had a new boyfriend. He was kind, he was adorable, my parents liked him, and he was crazy about me. Noah marked all the checkboxes.

The next weekend, Noah drove to Chicago and stayed at a nearby hotel. Since my kids were with me, we could only see each other when they weren't around, which meant dropping them off at their activities and meeting him for coffee, taking them to a friend's house for a couple hours while we went for a walk, and texting Noah when they fell asleep so that he could come over and watch a movie. All we did was kiss and snuggle. I felt like Noah was very serious about me. Our new relationship was nauseatingly adorable, and my friend Susan told me she was sure we'd get married.

Weekend number three was just as good. Noah came back to Chicago to see me. This time, my kids were with my ex for the weekend. We had a nice dinner date, went back to my house and watched a movie. Halfway through The Godfather, we started kissing on my couch. One thing led to another, and we slept together. The sex was good, but even better, I felt adored and secure. This guy really, really liked me. I fell asleep in Noah's arms happy and feeling safe. What happened next is something that would take years of therapy to figure out. I woke up feeling like something was wrong. Noah was trying to kiss me and be all lovey-dovey, and I felt suffocated, like I needed to get away. I couldn't breathe. Waking up with him didn't feel right. I was uncomfortable and I didn't want him here with me. I got into the shower and prayed to God to give me back the feelings I had for Noah—strong, loving feelings I had just hours ago. I wanted to love Noah so much. This was it. I had found the perfect husband. My kids would adore him, and I could start a new life with someone. Why was I pushing him away? When I walked out of the bathroom Noah was on the couch watching basketball.

"What's wrong?" he asked.

He wasn't mean or angry. He was too nice for that. Instead, he was concerned.

"I don't know what's wrong with me," I said.

"What time do you want to leave?" he asked.

"Wait, what?"

"For my parent's house. I told them we'd be there at 1:00 or 2:00.'

Maybe I'd had too much wine with dinner last night, but I completely forgot that I accepted Noah's invitation to have Sunday brunch with his mom and dad. My heart sank. While in the shower, I was thinking about how to break up with Noah, so how could I go to his parent's house and have a meal? There was no way.

I sat on the couch and started crying. Noah came and sat next to me. He put his hand on my wet hair. "Please tell me what's wrong."

I didn't answer for a long time because I was too scared to talk.

"I don't think I should go to your parent's house. I'm so sorry. I'm just not ready for this."

Noah looked like someone just punched him in the gut and at that moment, I could not have hated myself more.

"Ready for what? We can take things slower if you want."

I shook my head. "No. This doesn't feel right and if I meet your parents, it will be harder to end things."

Noah looked really sad and it made me sick. He tried talking to me more about my feelings, but I shut down, giving him one-word answers and a lot of awkward silence. He left a few minutes later. I still remember how relieved I was. It was like this huge burden had been lifted off of me. I was free. I didn't have to be worried or stressed anymore. It was done. Noah could meet a nice girl who wanted to eat lunch with his parents, and who wanted to get remarried and blend families. And me? I could go back to dating assholes who treated me like crap, so I wouldn't have to commit.

Looking back, I subconsciously turned myself off to Noah and to real love because I was a frightened, messed up woman with low self-esteem, who didn't think she was worthy of a relationship with a wonderful man and his wonderful family. Maybe it was because I hadn't done the work to heal myself from my divorce, or because I hadn't done the work to heal myself from issues that had been there my whole life. Whatever the reason, I had crushed Noah, and I will always feel badly about that. He was/is such a nice person, and he didn't deserve to have a girlfriend who dumped him right after they had sex, and right before she was supposed to meet his parents. Only a heartless bitch would do something like that, or someone who was really screwed up and whose self-worth was currently in the garbage can.

It is Noah who got the last laugh, however. My love life would continue to be a nightmare for years, while his would turn out blissful. Not surprisingly, he married a really nice, divorced woman with one child. I hear he is happy, and I am very pleased to know that. He deserves it. Additionally, Noah did extremely well professionally, which is also not surprising. He deserves that, too.

I have always wanted to apologize to Noah for hurting him. He's over me by now, obviously, but I always think that it might make him feel validated if he heard me tell him that it was me, not him; that I was screwed up and needed to get help and grow up, and that he could not have been a better boyfriend. Noah taught me a few things about love and self-love. First, if you are madly in love, and you suddenly feel suffocated and need space, look in the mirror and ask yourself, "why?" Because going from committed to non-committed so quickly has nothing to do with the other person and everything to do with your state of mind. Ask yourself why you are pulling away. Take some deep breaths and try to figure out what exactly is scaring you. Lastly, tell yourself you deserve this love. You are worthy of someone who is over-the-top in love with you, who wants to be with you every minute, and who wants to introduce you to his parents.

You Deserve to Be Deeply Loved

Self-love is a complicated thing. You can love parts of yourself and feel like you need to work on other parts, but emotionally healthy people who seek

40

out emotionally healthy relationships cut themselves a break and love all of themselves despite their many flaws and faults. Self-love means forgiving yourself for mistakes and acknowledging yourself for successes. It means treating yourself to food you love versus feeling guilty because of your unnecessary bad body image. It means taking trips to places you've never seen and buying yourself material things you really want instead of saving every penny of your hard-earned money because you feel guilty for spending it. Self-love means respecting yourself and being proud of who you are and how you live your life, doing the best you can, and not caring about other people's opinions. Self-love is looking in the mirror and telling yourself you deserve to be happy, and you deserve the love of others, including romantic love. It's getting your ex's words (and other toxic people's words) out of your head and listening to your own loving, caring words. Had I had all this wonderful insight while dating Noah, we would probably be married. Thank you for loving me, Noah. It was me, not you.

CHAPTER 5

The Rottweiler
(The Addict)

The Rottweiler is big, strong, and seemingly protective—until they feel you are threatening their space. Then they get aggressive and they bite. I'll show you my scar if you want.

Addiction is probably the hardest and most challenging relationship issue there is. Why? Because if you are in a relationship with an addict, you have no control over changing the addict's behavior, and most people cannot accept that. Therefore, the person who isn't the addict may find themselves attempting to help the addict by hiding the drug or alcohol, nagging the person to stop the behavior, or trying to reason with the person about why they need to stop, not fully comprehending that none of these things work.

Let me share something I learned when I spent some time in a relationship with Drew: You cannot make an addict want to get help. An addict has to decide he or she needs help and then commit to treatment and recovery. Not one person on Earth can make the decision to get clean or stay sober for them. Period. Much of my time spent with Drew was filled with fear, frustration and disappointment by his actions, and being angry with him because I felt like he was doing something wrong—which he was, and he wasn't.

As a great therapist once said to me, "Why are you angry with him? Would you be angry with him if he had cancer?"

"No," I replied.

"Alcoholism is an illness, just like any other illness, so try to think of it that way and you will probably find you aren't so angry," she said.

I spent years in therapy after dating Drew, trying to heal myself from the trauma and devastation of watching someone I deeply cared for destroy his life because of a terrible addiction.

Remember that when I dated Noah, he was too nice, and that I was used to dating men who treated me like crap? Well, I met Drew shortly after Noah. His addiction to alcohol made him severely dysfunctional and incapable of having a healthy romantic relationship, and yes, at times, he treated me like crap because he was drunk and abusive. I met Drew at a bar. Shocking. He was cute and charismatic. The reason for his divorce? In his words, "My wife wrote a best-selling cookbook, made a ton of money, and then decided she didn't want to be married anymore." I believed his story because I wanted it to be true. In hindsight, I bet his ex-wife was a really good person who just didn't want to be married to a drunk anymore.

Drew was like a big teddy bear. He was also a beer and pizza kind of guy, living his life like a kid who just graduated college with no responsibility except a job. He and his ex didn't have kids, he had never owned a home, and the highlight of his week was watching Sunday, Monday, and Thursday night football. I ignored all the red flags because I had this attraction to Drew's big brown eyes and my desire to save and change yet another divorced man with issues.

Our conversations were pretty superficial, and there was a lot of joking, laughing, and serious conversation avoidance. On our first dinner date, Drew must have ordered five or six beers. And that was just at dinner. Afterwards, we went to a local comedy club, where I lost count. Ten days into the relationship, I took Drew to a friend's holiday party, an event to which I'd planned to go solo. I felt so lucky to have ended up with a last-minute date who I knew my friends would think was darling. Because honestly, he was. Drew was kind and he was funny and warm and really down-to-earth. He was an amazing kisser, and I always felt so happy when we were together. Being with Drew was safe, because in the back of my mind, I knew this relationship was going nowhere, even though I wouldn't admit it. The party went fine, but shortly after that night, Drew decided to display his ugly colors.

We went out to dinner with my friend, Marcy, and her husband. They were a couple I had known for over 20 years, and I felt like they were the perfect people for our first double date. Marcy wasn't judgmental, and she and her husband were warm and welcoming, always making those they just met feel included. As usual, during the meal Drew drank several beers, and I could tell my friends were surprised at how quickly he was ordering and downing the drinks. I felt embarrassed.

We said our good-byes in the parking lot and walked to my car. When we got in, I asked, "Did you have fun?"

Drew was quiet.

"What is it?" I asked. "Is something wrong?"

"Honestly, I thought they were assholes."

My heart dropped. It wasn't just what he said, but Drew's tone was like that of the devil. It was cold and mean and distant.

I was so shocked I couldn't even respond.

"I mean, why would you want to even associate with those people?" he asked.

I still could not speak.

He started to get belligerent. "F*cking answer me," he said.

Now he reminded me of a mean, drunk guy, the kind of guy who gets sloppy and obnoxious and aggressive, and who no one wants to be around. He started going on and on about why he didn't like Marcy and why was I friends with them?

He proceeded to blurt out the dealbreaker. "You're just an idiot."

My jaw was on the ground, but I managed to keep driving. We got to Drew's house, and I stopped the car and said quietly, "Good night."

"What? You're not coming in? Great! F*cking leave. That's real mature. Whatever. You should go meet your asshole friends."

You might wonder why I just used the word dealbreaker, yet this chapter isn't nearly over. That's because what he said was the dealbreaker, and yet it wasn't. That's the difference between someone who understands addiction and someone who doesn't. At the time, I didn't grasp that his cruel, disrespectful insults were the drinks talking—his liquid devil. I didn't understand that he had lost control over his monster. Had I understood the disease, I would have ended the relationship that night. But I didn't. That's why there is more to this story.

After crying myself to sleep and telling myself that karma was getting back at me for breaking up with Noah, I was awakened around 7 a.m. by my doorbell ringing. I knew it was Drew and I was cringing. How dare he come over here after the way he'd acted last night. I was fuming. I looked at my phone and I had eight missed calls and a bunch of texts from him.

I answered the door. Standing there was a sad sight. Drew looked like he'd been crying.

"Jackie, I don't even know what to say. I'm so sorry."

I let him in, and he immediately took my hands and continued, "I was such a jerk. I have no idea why I would say those things to you. I was really drunk. I didn't mean any of them. I just felt like your friends didn't like me and maybe that's my own insecurity. Can you forgive me?"

"I saw a side of you last night that scared me. I hated that person."

"I know. I hate him, too. He's a dick. I'm not that person. I promise, it will never happen again."

I knew he needed to leave. I knew right then the relationship would never be healthy. I knew I deserved better. My head was spinning while I was trying to figure out how to get him out the door. Then, he dropped the bomb.

"Jackie," he said with tears in his eyes. "I think I love you."

Suddenly, I became the idiot he called me nine hours earlier. Why? Because only an idiot would decide to pretend that the previous night was a one-time thing, an isolated incident, and believe this guy who said the L word way too quickly.

This became the cycle that went on with Drew for a couple more weeks. If I had to describe it, I'd say we'd have a nice date, followed by a date in which Drew's drunk, bad behavior got the best of him. It was hard to comprehend. Drew could be funny and charming and kind and cute and affectionate, and then, he could just turn cruel out of nowhere. Drew drank on every date, of course. I tried to ignore it, but it made me uncomfortable because I was afraid he could turn into that jerk I hated any second. We would get into fights, and I would leave his house, and the next day, he'd come crawling back, apologizing, telling me he was going to stop drinking. That happened about three times.

During that short span, I began to feel like a battered wife. Honestly. I didn't know how to get out of the relationship. It almost felt like an obligation to stay with him. I felt guilty, like I would be abandoning him if I broke up with him. Self-hatred started to creep in. I also had no self-respect. How could I allow this man to treat me like this? It was awful. I lost a lot of weight because I couldn't eat. My stomach started hurting all the time. I distanced myself from my friends because I was too embarrassed to talk about my relationship and I knew it was bad. Very bad. I never, ever considered introducing him to my kids. Why would I want to expose them to such toxicity? Also, Drew and I never had sex. I never felt comfortable taking it to that level and honestly, I think Drew cared more about chugging beer than getting me into bed.

I took Drew to a friend's birthday party, and it was torturous. I was walking on eggshells the entire time because I didn't want to poke the drunk bear. I was afraid he would embarrass me. I hated myself more. Drew also had this friend, Ken, who he'd go out with and talk to me about. From day one, I thought Ken was a bad influence. Ken had actually been out with Drew the night we met, and I remember thinking Ken was one of those guys that no girl wanted her boyfriend to be friends with. He was a heavy drinker, a player, and had no respect for women. Ken was the kind of guy who would root for his buddy to dump you. But I faked it and only said nice things about him to Drew. There was a time Drew came over after a night out with Ken and threw up in my bathroom. There was a time he wanted to drive and I had to fight him for the keys. There were times he wasn't mean, just an annoying, sloppy drunk, who thought he was being funny. I tried talking to Drew about his drinking a couple of times.

"Would you consider getting some therapy?" I would ask. I never even mentioned treatment because I didn't understand that therapy alone won't make an addict quit the addiction.

"I don't need help, trust me," he said once.

Another time, he got really angry with me for even bringing it up. "You're the reason I drink," he said in a nasty tone. "Maybe I should break up with you. Then I won't drink anymore."

I knew talking about it was no longer an option. I also knew his drinking addiction wasn't my fault. The end of Drew and I came after what I recall as the worst night of my life. After being out with that loser, Ken, Drew was extremely intoxicated and came over to my house. I was less than thrilled about seeing him, and he didn't like that one bit. So, he started a fight with me, calling me the usual names: an idiot, cold bitch, and horrible person. Finally, I'd had it. I was done walking on eggshells.

"Get the hell out!" I shouted.

"Who are you to tell me what to do?" he yelled back.

He then walked towards me and that's when I got really, really scared. He grabbed my shoulders. "Huh? Who the f*ck are you?" he shouted while shook me. It really hurt.

"Get your hands off me!" I yelled.

Drew then pushed me across the room, and I fell onto the floor pretty hard.

"F*ck you, I'm out of here."

My heart was pounding, I was crying, and all I could think about was how much worse this could have been. He could have beaten me up. He could have killed me. I sat there crying for a long time. The next day, I noticed I had thumbprint bruises on my upper arms. I loathed Drew, but even more so, I loathed myself. That's when I started talking to the best therapist in the world about alcohol addiction. I actually spent several years learning about it and ended up attending Al-Anon. I don't know what made me decide to go, I just felt like a survivor and I felt compelled to be there. The first meeting, I cried the whole time, and a really nice lady came up to me afterwards and told me that everyone cries at their first meeting.

Drew tried to contact me a few times after that night, but I never responded. I was traumatized by my whole experience with him. It took me a very long time to come to terms with how I could have stayed in such a toxic relationship, even for the few weeks I did. That's why I never judge others in the same position. I did write him a letter a few years later, but I didn't send it. That actually was very therapeutic.

I truly believe that addictions are the devil, but here is the good news. First, I have never dated anyone again who had an addiction. The minute I would spot it, I would move on. I credit educating myself on the illness as the reason why. Secondly, I have met men and women over the years who are recovered addicts, and I always find that very refreshing and inspiring. One person was my friend's husband. I ran into him one day at Starbuck's and said hello, and he acted like he didn't know me.

"Joe, it's Jackie Pilossoph," I said.

He still didn't seem to know me.

"How can you not remember me? I've seen you and Emily out several times over the years and you've bought me drinks every time."

"Wow," said Joe. "I have to tell you, I'm so sorry. I don't even remember. I am an alcoholic, who was drinking back then. My wife told me if I didn't get help, I would have to move out, and that made me go to a treatment program. I didn't want to lose my wife and kids. I've been sober for three years, and it's still really hard every day, but it's worth the fight."

Right there in the middle of the Starbuck's line, I hugged Joe.

"Thank you for sharing that with me. It means a lot."

I have such compassion for addicts and maybe even more so for their spouses. My therapist once told me that there is no right or wrong answer when it comes to deciding if you should leave or stay with your spouse who is an addict. She said no one should judge your decision, and that some people stay forever, some leave right away, and others leave somewhere in between.

If you are currently with an addict who is not in treatment, I'm not saying it can't work out. What I will say is, the relationship will not be healthy until the addict admits he or she needs help and then gets help. My advice to the spouse is to completely stay out of it. That doesn't mean you can't be supportive while the addict is in treatment and after, but while the addict is still using, the spouse needs to realize they have no control over the addict, and that nothing they do will help. Hiding the drug or alcohol won't help. Pleading with the person to go into a treatment program won't help. Yelling at the person and telling them how bad it is for their health won't help. And threatening to leave won't help, although sometimes when a spouse leaves (like Joe's wife), that is the needed wake-up call for the addict to go into treatment. What you can do is talk to a therapist about having an intervention—a surprise meeting where you and your spouse's family and close friends approach your ex, tell the person they need to go into a treatment program, and then have it all set up so that the person can go straight there after the meeting. It's not easy to do, but in many cases, it is effective. Additionally, the spouse and children of an addict need to get help and support, such as therapy and/or Al-Anon, because the addict is affecting their lives, too, in a huge way.

I have no idea what happened to Drew. I don't know if he ever got help for his addiction. I know in my heart that he is a good person. He's a good person with a really, really bad problem. I really cared for him. But the fact is that alcoholism or any addiction is much bigger than a relationship. I can say firsthand, that love alone will not get a couple through addiction.

10 Things I know about alcoholism and addiction:

1. You have no control over your loved one's addiction, so stop trying to intervene, unless you feel that he or she or your kids or you are in danger.

2. You can try a group intervention, but just know that it might not work.

3. Your spouse isn't being mean to you because he or she is a bad person. The addiction is being mean to you.

4. Try not to be angry with your spouse because addiction is an illness, just like cancer, Parkinson's, or another disease.

5. Getting therapy and/or attending an Al-Anon meeting is one of the best things you can do. In fact, it is crucial to your emotional wellbeing.

6. If you ever feel you are in physical danger, you need to leave and bring your children with you.

7. If your ex says he or she is going to quit the addiction on their own, be supportive, but realize that it won't work.

8. Remember that his or her addiction is not your fault, even though they might say it is.

9. Talk to a therapist if you feel guilty for leaving an alcoholic. I understand how you feel, but you deserve happiness.

10. Forgive yourself if you feel you stayed too long. Forgive yourself if you feel you left too soon. Addiction is complicated. These decisions are very very hard decisions. You're doing the best you can.

CHAPTER 6

The Maltese
(The Vince Vaughn Look-alike)

The Maltese is playful, vigorous, and affectionate. While that's wonderful for a while, it has a shelf-life.

In every romantic relationship, both partners have an idea in the back of their minds about why they're in the relationship and what they want out of it. They might say they're not sure, and maybe they aren't, but deep down, they know, whether they admit it to themselves or not. Maybe you're dating the guy you think could be the one. Or you're with the cute, fun guy who is a better boyfriend than husband. Perhaps the relationship you're currently in is about amazing sex, but nothing else. There are no right or wrong reasons to be in a relationship. That's the beauty of dating.

What is wrong, however, is when you're with someone and you start lying to yourself about what the relationship really is and where it's going. You start rationalizing it and saying to yourself, "This can work." "We are going to be the exception." "I really, really love him." "I know he loves me, even though he doesn't say it." Sound familiar? Being dishonest with yourself about what your relationship really, truly is can only cause frustration and disappointment, and it taints the wonderful relationship you have or had. The key to staying happy in it and having an easier time letting go when it ends is admitting and accepting the truth about what is really going on in your relationship, and the expectations each of you have.

After Drew, I felt like I needed a break from men, so I didn't date for about six months. My focus was on healing from my divorce and taking care of my kids. I also continued my passion: writing. Every second I wasn't with the kids I was writing. I found such comfort and peacefulness in journaling my thoughts, which ended up being a large part of the first novel I ever wrote (which is still sitting in a drawer but that's OK). Writing was my stress outlet. It was therapeutic and it was working. I also continued therapy, went to some movies by myself, spent a ton of time walking alone, and had a few girl parties at my house with women from my neighborhood. I remember during that time I felt empowered and independent because I wasn't putting pressure on myself to find love. Instead, I was working on crafting a better, happier, simpler life. I was setting goals and I started to have dreams of becoming a published author.

But just as I was content being alone, I was sucked back into that darn suburban bar scene. It started with a phone call from my friend, Robin, a woman I had become friends with through our young kids. Her husband worked in management for a large corporation that was based in our town. He was taking his team out for a happy hour on a Wednesday night.

"It's going to be all guys and I don't want to be the only girl," said Robin. "Will you meet me there?"

My kids had just left for a four-day weekend with my ex. The party sounded fun, and harmless, and I really liked Robin, so I accepted. I knew all the guys were going to be in their twenties and thirties, so I wasn't expecting to meet anyone, which everyone knows is exactly when you do meet someone. A few minutes after walking in, Robin handed me a beer and then continued to mingle with her husband's staff. There I stood, all alone. I wasn't nervous or insecure, though, because I truly didn't care. I was in a great place: confident, self-sufficient, and on my way back to professional success. But then, right at the moment when I felt like I didn't care if I ever met another man again, I saw Jeff.

Standing a few feet away from me talking to a group of people, he was a double for Vince Vaughn in Swingers. He was tall, dark, and hot, not to mention more than a decade younger than I was. He kept looking over at me and smiling, and I thought it was kind of funny. I seriously didn't know why he was focused on me. A couple minutes later he walked over to me.

"Hi," he said. "I'm Jeff." He extended his hand.

All of a sudden, my heart started to pound. Was he flirting with me?! We started talking and I found out he was from Michigan, had been with his company in a finance role for a few years, and the funniest thing: he was looking forward to celebrating his 30th birthday!

He was adorable. He was beautiful, but he was also young and a little bit shy. I told him about my divorce, my kids, and my pre-marriage careers, which included pharmaceutical sales representative and TV reporter. I also told him I was a writer, which at this point I officially was. An hour later, I thought it was time for me to go home.

"OK, I'll walk you to your car," he said, already leading me out of the crowd. He was walking so fast that I didn't even say goodbye to Robin. The walk was silent, and the next time Jeff spoke was when we got to my car. "Can I get in?" he asked.

I didn't answer, I just popped the locks with my key fob and Jeff opened the door and got into the passenger seat. Horrified by empty sippy cups, plastic containers filled with Goldfish, and two car seats strapped in the back, I started giggling.

"What's so funny?" Jeff asked.

Still laughing, I declared, "I think we're about to make out."

Jeff chuckled and then he began kissing me. Let me tell you, it was good. Really good. Vince, I mean Jeff, was 12 years younger than me, he was gorgeous, he smelled great, and he had this innocence that was beyond appealing.

Did I say innocence? After several minutes Jeff whispered, "Can I come home with you?"

"Yeah, um… that won't work. This has been really fun, though," I said in an attempt to ease how awkward things had just gotten.

Jeff laughed and said, "Give me your phone."

"Why?"

"Just give it to me."

I handed him my phone him and watched him put his number in it. He then called himself with my phone and hung up. I got such a kick out of this. Remember, this was 2010 and iPhones were still relatively new back then. I had a Blackberry, which I didn't even know how to use completely, so I didn't know that this was how people got each other's numbers.

"You seem really good at this," I said. "You must do it often."

"Not as often as you think," he replied. Then he kissed me goodnight and got out of the car. On the drive home, I was smiling so much my cheeks were hurting.

He texted me goodnight, and the next day he texted asking if I wanted to go out for dinner that night. The first thing I did was call Robin.

"Hi, what are you up to?" I asked.

"Not getting ready for a date with Jeff," she answered.

I was shocked. He had apparently already called Robin and her husband and told them his plans to ask me out.

"Should I go?" I asked her. "I'm scared."

"Of course you should go," she said. "He's a really sweet guy."

"He's a teenager."

"Are you looking to get remarried right now?"

I couldn't argue with that statement, so I texted back and at 7:30 p.m., Jeff picked me up and the cougar and her date drove to dinner.

We ate crab cakes, a salad, and we split a steak. We also had a bottle of Pinot Noir, and a couple hours later we were at my place. Passionate kissing began in the laundry room, where we entered my house. Clothes started coming off as we made our way into the living room, up the stairs and to my bedroom. We never made it to my bed. We made love on the carpet in the hallway. Yes, I used a condom. I had actually gone out and bought some that day. That's how much I knew that this was going to happen.

We eventually got into my bed and talked and laughed and snuggled. Jeff slept on my stomach for a little while, which actually made me like my stomach for the first time in my life. This darling guy somehow managed to make me feel good about my body just the way it was at 43 years old. It was what he said and the way he whispered things. "I love your skin." "You have the best eyes." "Do you believe me? You should."

After a while, Jeff told me he was hungry. He thew on his boxers, I picked up his t-shirt in the hallway and put in on, and we headed downstairs to the kitchen. Snacking on leftover pasta, cheese and crackers, and grapes, we talked and laughed in between gulps of water (the kids' apple juice for him). I remember that night as being one of the most romantic, fun times I've ever had.

Over the next several weeks it went like this: Jeff would always text first and ask when I was available, and then we would go on a date—either out for dinner or to my house, where we would cook and drink wine. And then, Jeff would text a few days later to make plans again. He never called just to talk, and he never emailed me. I remember daydreaming a lot that summer. I'd be playing in the pool with my kids, and then while drying off and soaking up the sun I'd find myself thinking about this passionate romance I had going on that no one knew about. The sex became almost addictive, and there were times I didn't like how desperate I felt to see Jeff again. When I met him, I had finally come to this place of self-sufficiency, like I didn't need to be in a relationship to be happy. I didn't want to lose that. Then again, I could never remember feeling so good around someone.

What was refreshing was that Jeff didn't have any baggage. How could he? He was 29, came from a nice family, had gone to a good college, had a great job, and had never really had a serious girlfriend. There was such simplicity about him, and I don't mean that in a condescending way. Being simple doesn't mean he wasn't intelligent or that he didn't have deep feelings, he was just trouble-free and humble, despite his striking looks and professional success. An older person who is divorced has more stories, more depth. That doesn't make one person better than the other, just different.

I started to think that maybe I could make this work. Why couldn't an almost 30-year-old and a 43-year-old end up together? Demi and Ashton had done it. Their age difference was about the same as ours, and it had worked out wonderfully (so I thought at the time). I began fantasizing about us getting more serious, falling in love, and moving him in to live with me and the kids. They would love him. It could work, I told myself. So, I decided to put it to the test. One day, I texted Jeff and asked if he wanted to plan a trip together. Maybe we could go to Vegas or even Wisconsin to see how we'd be spending a few days together non-stop. Jeff never answered the text, and when we got together, I asked him about it.

"Yea, sorry I didn't respond," he said. "I'm kind of busy every weekend for the next few weekends. Sorry."

My heart sank because that was the exact moment I realized that I was just a fling for Jeff. Not that he didn't care about me or respect me or treat me great. He did. But he didn't want anything I had been dreaming about recently. And the thing was, I don't even think it was my age or the fact that I had kids. He didn't want a serious commitment with me or anyone else. Jeff liked being single and he liked his lifestyle. Now I had to come to terms with the fact that our relationship wasn't going to last very much longer. I could see it winding down. We weren't going to fall in love and get married like the Kutchers. And honestly, I knew in my heart that I didn't want to marry Jeff either. I had taken this wonderful relationship and tried to make it into something it just wasn't.

Shortly after the trip conversation, I wasn't surprised that Jeff started to text less and our dates became more about hooking up. It was apparent that he felt pressured and was backing off. Emptiness began to creep in, and I didn't like it. I felt a bit used and started to resent Jeff a little. Because I didn't want to have those feelings and because I knew deep down they weren't justified, I decided to break up with him. Since we had had such a great run, I didn't want things to get ugly. It was just too sweet of a romance to ruin with a bitter breakup. What was there to be bitter about? Nothing. I called him. I think it was the first time we had ever talked over the phone. Before now, everything had been communicated via text, talk, or love making. He was surprised to hear from me but seemed very happy. So happy, in fact, that I almost backed out of the breakup.

"To what do I owe this phone call?" he asked.

"I don't think we should see each other anymore."

Jeff seemed shocked. "Why?"

"Because I want a boyfriend," I said. "I want someone who wants to take me on vacation or to parties, or who wants to go out for dinner with my girlfriends and their husbands. I don't want to have to hide."

"I'm not hiding, are you?"

"Jeff, I asked you to go on vacation and you freaked."

"I didn't freak."

"Do you want to take me out with your friends and their girlfriends? Do you want to meet my parents? Even better, do you want to be a stepdad?"

"You're the one who said you don't want a serious relationship," he said.

"I don't, but I don't want this either." Suddenly, I started to cry.

"Are you crying?"

"No, why would you say that?"

Suddenly, he seemed really concerned. "Oh my God, please don't cry."

"I'm not crying. Listen, I have to go. My daughter's calling me," I lied. "I have to go see what she needs."

I think Jeff was sad and so was I. There were no bad feelings, no negative words, and only memories that made me feel good, and that made me smile, which made this ending even harder. For example, to this day, I still laugh about the time I bought a new purse.

I asked Jeff, "Do you think this looks too much like a diaper bag?"

His response: "What's a diaper bag?"

In the days and weeks that followed our breakup, the times I cried about Jeff didn't feel awful, I just missed him, and I missed what we had. And I also felt heartbroken. Again. Another loss. More loneliness. I've heard from therapists that when people get divorced and then get into their first semi-serious relationship, they are devastated when that relationship ends. Why? Because it brings back the feelings of loss that they had from the marriage ending. Experiencing the pain of another breakup can be almost more painful than the divorce.

Over time, I began to heal, and the feelings of sadness were replaced more and more with the gratitude I felt for what Jeff did for me: He made me feel young and sexy, he was respectful, he adored me, and he gave me the memory of moments that are indescribably precious. What beautiful gifts. How can you be sad or regret that? You can't.

What's important to remember is, if you're in a relationship that you know in your heart is going to be short-term, don't try to make it something it isn't. Don't fantasize that you and your guy are going to be the exception, that you are going to spend the rest of your lives together, that you will make it work, and that people will all be shocked. All that does is cause unrealistic expectations and self-induced pressure, which lead to disappointment, which then taints the wonderful relationship you have or had. Why not walk away when you know the time is right—before arguments and resentment begin to creep in?

After a few months, Jeff and I were able to become platonic friends and we stayed in touch for a long time. We reached out on each other's birthdays, and at one point, he asked me for relationship advice. It was ironic. He was seeing a woman with two young kids. I never think about the disappointment I started to feel at the end of our relationship, but instead I recall a physically gorgeous, sweet younger man who made me really happy for a little while, and who gave me hope that love and romance after divorce are possible. Jeff got married a few years ago. He was 43 at the time, the same age I was when I met him. When I saw his wedding pictures on Facebook, I found myself both a teeny tiny bit jealous and very happy for him. He and his wife looked adorable.

How do you know when it's time to end your fling?

1. You buy a new dress, only to be disappointed by him walking in the door and immediately taking it off of you rather than taking you out for dinner.

2. Resentment starts to creep in because you know in your heart he's flirting and maybe even dating other women.

3. You've asked him to take a weekend trip with you and he keeps saying, "Ummm…yeah, let me get back to you on that."

4. The sex spark starts to diminish. It's hard to recreate the electricity, newness, and intensity of the first few weeks.

5. You realize he's a genius at changing the subject every time the conversation remotely heads towards your relationship or future together.

6. Hearing about another one of his crazy nights out with the guys makes you roll your eyes.

7. You start to feel a little bit used, even if you suspect you might be using him, too.

8. You think, "How could I not have seen how immature and childish he is?"

9. You wish you could package and freeze those first few dates, when the two of you couldn't get enough of each other.

10. Your gut is telling your heart to accept that your fling isn't the love of your life.

Still liking the book? Check out the Divorced Girl Smiling Website!

CHAPTER 7

The Jack Russell Terrier (The Cheater)

The Jack Russell Terrier loves to dig and is full of mischief. Unfortunately, I looked the other way and let him get into all kinds of trouble for way too long.

Being cheated on might be the most painful thing that can happen to someone in a relationship. Whether you suspected it or you were blindsided, finding out your partner was unfaithful triggers so many different emotions: shock, devastation, disgust, anger, self-doubt, and more.

It is true that some couples are able to work things out and stay together after infidelity, but I think more times than not, trust is broken and can't be repaired. I mean, if you gave a cheater a second chance, wouldn't you always be wondering who that late-night text is from, or why he came home later than usual from work last night, or what he's really up to on an out-of-town business trip? I'm not saying a relationship can't work out after cheating, but I think infidelity puts a stain on a couple that will always be noticeable by both partners.

After Jeff, I took another dating break—this time not by choice. To say I was in a dating dry spell is putting it mildly. I basically couldn't get a date to save my life. Dating dry spells are tough. They can feel lonely, they can make you feel undesirable and unwanted, and they can cause you to lose hope that you will ever find the one, simply because in order to find the one you actually have to go on dates! But the one thing I know about dry spells is that they always end. And when they end, you can be sure something really exciting is on the horizon. After my dry spell ended, I went out with a few dogs, who don't really deserve entire chapters dedicated to them. They included:

1. The Chihuahua (The Pinecone)

The Chihuahua is lively and very devoted—in this case, he was still desperately in love with and devoted to his ex-wife, which is why he bounced around from relationship to relationship, and could not commit to anyone, including me.

2. The Shih Tzu (The "Honey We're Out of Milk Guy")

The Shih Tzu is intelligent, playful, social, and unfortunately, mischievous. While on a date with him, a text popped up on his iPhone that read "Honey, we're out of milk. Want me to pick some up?" After squirming for a few seconds, he fessed up and told me he was dating other women to figure out if he was really serious about wanting to get divorced.

3. The Pug (The Protégé)

The Pug is sociable, a good companion, and loves to mooch off others, including moi. I took this divorced dad under my wing by coaching him in the interview process to land a high-level, high-paying medical sales job. He ended up getting the job, which he got fired from after a week because they felt he was underqualified, i.e., he didn't have me there to do the job for him. He ended up dumping me because he said he "wasn't feelin' it."

Considering giving up on men for good, I reluctantly agreed to go on a blind date with Derrek. The guy who set me up was a guy I met in a bar, who is actually a really sweet guy, and to this day, it makes me happy to run into him. I wish I could say the same for Derrek.

Derrek had been separated for about a year, but his divorce wasn't finalized yet. I didn't think much of it. After all, the divorce process can take a long time, months, even years sometimes, so why should it matter if someone isn't technically divorced yet, right? Wrong. After two dinner dates, Derrek and I started seeing each other a lot. I can't say I was head over heels in love, but he was kind, plus he had this really soft hair and I enjoyed running my fingers through it while making out with him. A couple months into the relationship, Derrek took me to his best friend's son's Bar Mitzvah, where I first met his soon-to-be ex-wife, Emma. Thin, blonde, and beautiful, I was extremely intimidated by her physically. When she introduced herself, she was friendly, but almost overly enthusiastic, as if she was trying to compensate for something. I had no clue what that was all about, and I felt nervous the whole time.

When I look back on my three-year relationship—yes, I said three years—with Derrek, I truly think I was blind. I didn't let myself see every sign there was to see that Derrek would have gotten back together in a heartbeat with Emma the entire time if she wanted it. First there was his daughter's band concerts. About every other week, he'd tell me he couldn't get together tonight because his daughter had a band concert he had to attend. I didn't realize he was lying until a few years later when my own daughter started playing the flute, and there were two band concerts the entire school year. Then there was the income tax issue. Every year, he and Emma would get together to do their taxes. Who the f*ck does their taxes year-after-year with their ex-spouse, who they intend to get divorced from? Isn't that what accountants are for? And, in this day and age of the Zoom and e-filing, why is there a need for an in-person meeting? Why? Sex. But every time I'd bring up my concerns to my boyfriend, he'd say something like, "Are you really going to be that insecure, paranoid girlfriend?" or "The reason I love you so much is because you are confident. Don't be that needy girl," or my favorite one, "I am not attracted to her at all. The thought of having sex with her makes me want to vomit." So, I'd end up brushing off my suspicions and being disappointed in myself for being so insecure. But perhaps the biggest sign I missed when it came to Derrek and Emma's sex life behind my back was when the two actually took a trip together!

About a year into our relationship, I was sitting at a restaurant in the city having lunch with Derrek when his wife called and told him their daughter had broken her arm at summer camp. After a short conversation with her, he told me he had to leave, and that he and Emma were driving to the camp in a few hours. Wait, what? My boyfriend was driving six hours with his ex-wife?

"Where are you staying?" I asked him.

"At a hotel."

"The same hotel?!"

"Why are you worried about that?" he asked. "Are you that insecure?"

"You're getting your own room, obviously. Right? Please tell me you're getting your own room."

"Look, I'm not going to spend the money for two hotel rooms," he replied.

I knew he was cheating. I so f*cking knew. Yet, I decided to tell myself that I was being ridiculous, that they were only going there for the benefit of their daughter and that I needed to get a grip and think of the kid, not myself.

About year later, Emma met a man, fell in love, and got engaged. All of a sudden, after years of dating Derrek, his divorce was becoming finalized. What a coincidence. (That was sarcastic.) Emma ended up getting married right around the time Derrek started giving me an ultimatum to get married. It was then that because of my indecision, we fell apart. In the end, we both knew things weren't working out, so we broke up and got back together a few times and finally ended our relationship. But that's not the end of my Derrek story.

When you spend three years with someone, it's pretty hard to just walk away. Regardless of the resentment I felt for many things that had transpired, I had a lot of sentimental feelings towards Derrek, and I wanted to remain friends with him, sincerely. So, after we broke up, we'd talk on the phone every now and then, and during the conversations, we'd rehash some of the things that happened in our long relationship and why it didn't work out. A few months later, I began dating someone new. I was crazy about him, and Derrek sensed it. I could tell he was angry and resentful that I was so happy. Don't get me wrong, he had been seeing someone new too, but I don't think he was optimistic about it working out. One day, Derrek and I were on the phone having a conversation and it turned into an argument. We said some really mean things to each other; things that needed to come out. There was obviously some pent-up resentment and hostility on both ends, which is understandable. But then, all of a sudden, Derrek blurted out, "Oh, and I slept with Emma the whole first year we were together."

Suddenly I felt the earth give out beneath me. "What?" I asked with trepidation.

"You heard me," he said in a cold, callous voice.

I realized that what my ex-boyfriend just said to me was information I already knew. I had always known it. But now it wasn't my gut assuring me I was cheated on; it was a fact.

"Why are you telling me this now?" I asked.

He answered, "Because I want you to hurt as much as I do."

In an instant, I was insanely furious, but I was also feeling a strange tinge of delight, stemming from the fact that I now had validation about something: I wasn't crazy! All those times I felt annoyed with myself for being insecure and not having faith in Derrek and his word, I was actually right! But that thought made me even angrier. How could he allow me to doubt myself, to feel needy and insecure, when in fact my feelings were warranted?! I was so angry, I could barely breathe, and not just for that night. I stayed mad for an entire summer. Had I found out about the cheating at the time, I could have saved myself years! We'd have broken up right then. Instead, I spent so much time living a lie and thinking Derrek was in love with me, when in reality he still loved his ex-wife. He only wanted to marry me to become someone else's husband, in the hope that a new wife would mend his broken heart. I'm sure of it. Try living with that feeling. It's not easy, even today.

In the days following the big reveal, I acted a little bit psychotic. I called his friends, his family, I even called Emma! No one wanted to get into it with me, which was hurtful, but now I get it. People don't want to get involved in another couple's web of cheating, lies, and heartbreak.

Emma's response was, "You should really talk to Derrek about this. Oh, and I would appreciate this not ending up in the Chicago Tribune." Well, that's all I had to hear. At the time, I was writing a weekly a column called "Love Essentially" that was published in a local paper which was owned by the Chicago Tribune. It was also published in the Chicago Tribune and all Tribune-owned papers across the country. Almost every column I wrote that summer had to do with cheating, trust, and loyalty. "What to do after the cheating," "Cheating is bad, but cruelty is worse," "Can you trust others after you've been cheated on?" and "Advice for those who have been cheated on" were just a few titles. Piss off a journalist and that's the price you pay. I remember people saying to me, "Glad you're not mad at me," fearing I would write about them, as well. My response has always been, "If you don't act like a dick, you have nothing to be worried about."

One last really interesting part of this story is that a few years later, I met the owner of the camp where Derrek and his wife went to pick up their daughter. She ended up telling me that she offered Derrek and his wife complimentary separate rooms and that he declined!

Finding out you've been cheated on can make you feel a mix of emotions:

1. Naïve
2. Stupid
3. Hopeless
4. Angry
5. Resentful
6. Vengeful
7. Relieved
8. Validated

Being the victim of infidelity taught me many valuable lessons. First, if you suspect someone is cheating, they are. For sure, 100%, no questions asked. Don't beat yourself up and tell yourself you are insecure and needy, and that this is about your self-confidence because it isn't.

Three words: He. Is. Cheating.

Secondly, if someone chooses to make you think you are paranoid and insecure by a cheating accusation instead of fessing up to the cheating, the gaslighting is just coldhearted, cowardly, and cruel. Not only are they deceiving you, but they are destroying your self-confidence, causing you self-doubt, and making you an unhappy person at the expense of their selfishness. The lying is worse than the cheating, in my opinion. Furthermore, if the person comes out and tells you about the cheating just to hurt you, that person is a mean-spirited, dirty fighter and you should stay as far away as possible. In other words, being friends isn't the best option.

When I look back on the three years of my life with Derrek, I think to myself that three years is truly a long time to spend in a romantic relationship. It's hard to believe with so many doubts about the relationship and a clear lack of trust that it lasted for so long. But in a way, maybe I subconsciously knew it wasn't right, and wasn't ready for Mr. Right, so I chose not to stir the pot.

Perhaps the saddest part about this whole story is that for me, when I think about Derrek, the cheating is what I will remember most, specifically Derrek's effort to put the feelings of distrust onto me, to make me feel like it was my issue. You just don't do that to someone you love, and you don't do that if you are a loving person. You just don't.

It's been several years since I've talked to or seen Derrek or Emma, and to be honest, I'm not sure how I would feel if I ever bumped into them. I'm not angry anymore, but I will always be hurt. Lesson: Healing after infidelity takes a lot of time and self-reflection. And remember, not everyone cheats.

Is He a Cheater? 13 Red Flags:

1. He turns his phone over before putting it down on a table.
2. You've never met any of his family or friends.
3. The two of you are not connected on social media—not even LinkedIn.
4. He is unavailable for long periods of time, either to talk or text.
5. Your gut tells you something's wrong.
6. He seems cocky, like if you broke up it wouldn't be that big of a deal.
7. He closes doors when on the phone.
8. No future plans are made. Everything is kind of last minute.
9. He seems nervous when his phone dings or rings.
10. He is using his laptop, and he closes it when he sees you walk towards him.
11. Your friends tell you they don't trust him.
12. He gaslights you--accuses you of cheating or sneaking around.
13. He blames your suspicion on you being insecure and/or needy.

If you like the book, you'll love the Divorced Girl Smiling Podcast!

CHAPTER 8

The Beagle
(My Mr. Big)

The Beagle is happy-go-lucky, easygoing, and fun. Described by some as "merry," they have tons of energy and can seem larger than life. My Mr. Big seemed that way to me.

I absolutely love having platonic friendships with men. I've felt that way my entire life—before I got married, while I was married, and after I got divorced. For example, I have a friend named Jack with whom I spent a lot of time in my twenties and thirties. Jack was and still is very nice looking and we had a lot in common, but we've never been anything more than platonic friends. During our friendship, Jack and I would go to the movies, out for dinner, or jogging. There was never any spark. Our friendship worked so well because of likeability and comfort, never mind the sad fact that we started to become the only two single people we knew, as all of our friends started dropping out of the singles scene to get married. Jack and I got to be so close that we would talk about our love lives and give each other relationship advice.

We both got married within a year of each other and sort of lost touch because Jack's wife doesn't like me. It's a bummer, but I would never want to cause any marital issues for anyone, so I keep my distance. Same story with another male platonic friend of mine named Burt. The only difference is, Burt and I dated for a few months before becoming genuine friends. Burt is also married, and his wife doesn't like me either. That said, I can sort of understand how she might feel uncomfortable since Burt and I dated. Honestly, though, it's such a shame. I miss being friends with those guys.

Say what you want about my now ex-husband, Charlie, but one thing he did that I thought was very cool was that he was supportive of me being to be friends with other men, even ex-boyfriends. Actually, Jack and Burt were both invited to our wedding (with dates, mind you). One thing I remember clearly was that when we were married and our son was about a year old, an old boyfriend of mine named Nick was in Chicago for work and asked if I wanted to get together for dinner. I asked my Charlie if he wanted to get a babysitter and join us. His response: "Hell no."

The night of the dinner, Nick came upstairs to see my son and meet my husband, who pretended to be on a work call the entire six minutes Nick was in the apartment. After dinner, Nick walked me back to my building and then caught a cab. The funniest part of this story is that when I got up to the apartment, the TV was on—the channel showing the security camera that was in front of the building. I thought it was cute that Charlie was spying on me. At that point, my marriage was still very good, so there was no insecurity. It was really nice.

My platonic friendships with men kicked in more than ever when I got divorced. There's something about divorced men and women living in the small suburban fish tank that keeps us bonded. Perhaps it's a commonality and an unspoken understanding of each other's states-of-mind that connects us. My first few years of being divorced, I met so many guys who I thought were kind and funny and fun, and with whom I enjoyed having a glass of wine and sharing stories. Most of these guys were harmless. There was no ulterior motive, meaning they weren't trying to date me or sleep with me. Don't get me wrong, one word of encouragement and they would have jumped. I'm not saying that in a conceited way, I just think they were lonely. But sex or no sex, I think everyone liked the feeling of being around other people who were going through what they were going through. It wasn't a pity party by any means, but rather an escape. The suburban divorcee bar crowd was happy and relaxed—for a few hours anyway. I'm pretty sure that when most people got home, many of those typical divorce feelings re-surfaced: sadness, fear, anxiety, and anger.

I can't even remember how or when I met Maria, a divorced dentist with two pre-teens. Maria was so cute. She was full of energy and smiles, and always had a positivity about her that was extremely attractive to me. I put Maria's contact info in my phone and vice versa, and she would text me if she was going to be out at the bars. If I got a text from her and didn't have my kids that night, I would go meet her, along with some of our other mutual divorced friends.

One night, I showed up at a local bar after getting a text from Maria declaring, "It's my birthday. Please meet me for a drink." When I walked in, it was crowded and loud, just a typical Thursday night for the divorced suburbanites. I looked around the bar and saw Maria standing around a bar table with a few people, including a couple other people I knew and liked. I saw shot glasses on the table, and I could hear them all laughing. But then, I noticed this one man who suddenly made the room fall silent. Everything froze and all I could focus on was him. I had never seen him before. He was nice-looking and seemed a little older. My reaction was kind of like the one you have when you see a celebrity in person. I was inexplicably stunned. I realized that this must be the guy Maria had been seeing and talking about—the guy who had been divorced forever and who wouldn't commit. According to her, it was a tortuous relationship. Seeing him made that statement make sense. My fascination was making me dizzy. Right then, I felt like Carrie Bradshaw the first time she ever saw Mr. Big. This guy was just like him—magnetic and exciting. I was dying to find out more.

"Jackie!" exclaimed Maria. "I'm so glad you came! Come over here and help us finish these shots."

I hugged her, wished her a happy birthday, and handed her the token birthday gift every divorced woman buys another divorced woman: a bottle of red wine with a bow around it. Then, I started saying hello and hugging everyone at the table. When I got to Mr. Big, I just said, "Hi." I was praying I didn't sound like a high school cheerleader saying hi to the quarterback. That's how it felt.

Before he could say anything, Maria exclaimed, "This is Scott. Scott, this is my friend, Jackie."

He smiled. I found myself so giddy that I truly felt like an idiot. We shook hands and just when I thought I couldn't love him anymore, he spoke. He had this great voice, sexy and confident. At this moment, I was sure he had been the school quarterback back in the day. Maria must have been reading my mind because she wasted no time explaining to Scott that I had a boyfriend. I had been dating Derrek (the Cheater) for about a year at the time. Looking back, I should have realized that my reaction to meeting Scott was a huge sign that I wasn't in a healthy place when it came to my relationship. I wasn't sure if it was wishful thinking, or if Scott looked disappointed by the news.

"So, how did you guys meet?" I asked.

"A friend of mine used to work for Scott," Maria gushed.

She was suddenly bugging me. I could not believe it, but I was jealous. I wanted to be Maria. I wanted to be Scott's girlfriend, second wife actually. Why was I feeling this way? What was wrong with me? Deep down I knew what was wrong with me. I had a boyfriend who was cheating on me, but in retrospect, I buried that gut instinct deeper than deep because of comfort and laziness. I left the bar that night with mixed emotions. Part of me was so excited to have met a guy like Scott. But at the same time, I felt confused and guilty, not to mention super envious of Maria.

"She isn't that good of a friend," I rationalized to myself. "When they break up, I can start dating him and just sort of lose touch with her."

About a week later, I met Maria for a drink, and the second I saw her I sensed something was wrong. She wasn't her usual, bubbly self but instead somber and anxious.

"Scott and I broke up again," she said. "We just don't want the same things."

"Oh, I'm so sorry to hear that. Are you OK?" I asked, while feeling like a piece of shit because I was secretly elated by the news. Only partially, though. I do have a heart, and I felt sad for Maria. She seemed genuinely heartbroken. She told me several stories that night about how this wasn't the first time they'd broken up because he'd either tell her he wanted to date someone else, or that he didn't want a girlfriend. But then he'd call her and say he made a mistake, and they'd pick up right where they left off, only with a little less trust and a little more resentment on her part. I really didn't like or trust Scott anymore, and I didn't like or trust me, either. Believe it or not, I still had this desire to get to know him better. Maybe he was a really good guy but wasn't in the right frame of mind for a girlfriend right now. Or maybe Maria wasn't the one. Maybe he wouldn't be like this if he was dating me. What a complete dick I was being. I ended up consoling Maria and decided to let it go with Scott and appreciate my current boyfriend. Weeks went by, and I moved on. But Scott was on my mind a lot more than I expected.

A couple months later, I was at a bar with my friend Susan, and guess who walks in? Scott and a friend of his. I couldn't believe it. Here he was in the flesh, and Maria was completely out of the picture! But Derrek wasn't. Oh, did I feel like a complete jerk. I waved and when Scott saw me, he came right over to our table.

"Jackie, right?" he asked with a huge smile.

I'm serious when I say that he seemed overjoyed to see me. Things were progressing nicely. I introduced him to Susan, and they shook hands. I could tell she found him as hot as I did. How could you not? He introduced us to the guy he was with, who seemed sweet enough.

"So, are you still dating your boyfriend?" he asked. That was his first question, and confirmation that chemistry is never one-sided.

It killed me to tell the truth. "Yes." I wanted to add, "Are you upset about that? Because say the word and I'll break up with him tonight."

"That's good," he responded. His insincerity was obvious.

As the drinks came and the loud music continued and more single divorced people entered the bar, something started happening and it was pissing me off. Susan and Scott began flirting with each other, to the point where they seemed like they were on a date, and I was stuck with the sweet guy. At the end of the night, after the sweet guy left, I had to cash in my chips and leave the happy couple at the bar. It was bothering me so much, but I knew I didn't have the right to be upset. I hated myself for being so disloyal to Derrek, but I hated Scott even more for coming into my life and confusing me. As I was leaving, he did something that doubled my confusion, but in a good way. He pulled me aside and said, "Hey, give me your number. Then I can text you when I'm going out and you can do the same."

We put each other's numbers in our phones, and it was then that I realized Scott liked me. He wanted to get to know me to keep his options open should Derrek and I ever break up. I actually thought the idea was genius. I could be platonic friends with Scott. How perfect was that? I could meet him out and I wouldn't be cheating, and I could get to know him and see how things went. I knew something was about to happen with him and Susan and I didn't like it, but now at least I was in the door, in a way.

The next day, Susan sent me a text that was oozing with excitement and joy: she was going out with Scott on Saturday night and get this—he was taking her on his boat! I told her I was happy for her. I didn't mention that I was sad for myself. After exchanging numbers with Scott, I felt kind of special, and deep down I knew that if I wasn't in a relationship, things would be different. A couple days before the big date, Susan called me and asked if I thought she should tell Maria she was going out with Scott. After all, they were friends. Not good friends, but Susan thought it was the right thing to do and I supported her. What happened next still makes me sad to this day. Apparently, the conversation with

Maria didn't go well. After Susan sprung the news, Maria responded, "That's fine. He'll never commit to you. He just wants to sleep with you."

Susan's ego was badly bruised, and she and Maria never spoke again. Maria stopped calling me, as well, I think because she assumed I was taking Susan's side. It was a little bit hurtful, but I learned something about divorce friendships: They can be special and meaningful in the moment, and a divorced friend will have your back like no one else in certain situations. But divorced friendships are much more volatile, and they tend to be shorter-lived. I guess you could say the friendships can be circumstantial. When people get over their divorces and move on, they sometimes realize they have nothing in common with the same people who were their lifesavers during that brutally painful time.

The day after the big date, Susan called me gushing. She said she had the best time, that Scott wined and dined her, and get this—that they had amazing sex. I was shocked. I guess I didn't know Susan as well as I thought. Still, I was happy if she was happy. But three days later when Scott hadn't called her, Susan's ego took another hit, and she was pissed. She apparently ended up calling Scott and yelling, "How dare you…" and some other stuff. I didn't see the point of her calling him, and I felt like asking her what she expected. Leopard? Spots? You get it. She knew who she was going out with, she wasn't born yesterday, and she slept with him anyway.

A couple days later, I was helping my kids with their homework when I got a text from Scott saying he was going to a bar close to my house and why don't I meet him? I was happy about it, but I also realized I was getting into the emotional cheating arena. That night, my kids were having dinner at my ex's and Derrek was playing in a men's basketball league game, so I figured it was meant to be. I couldn't ask Susan to go, so I would have to go by myself, which I obviously didn't mind.

When I walked in, Scott was sitting at the bar by himself. I walked up and said hi and gave him a hug that felt kind of awkward. This felt wrong. What was I doing? What if one of Derrek's friends saw me and thought I was cheating? Was I cheating? The next hour felt like a combination of a first date and a job interview. There wasn't a lot of flirting, and looking back, I think both of us were sizing the other up, figuring out what we wanted to be to each other: friends, lovers, nothing? There was no mistaking that Scott was attractive, but I also liked him as a friend. I found him very smart, and he had real life experience. He had traveled and owned businesses and made investments and had grown children. He wasn't a boy, he was man. He told great stories about places he'd been, real estate properties he owned, and other very grownup topics. I told Scott I could only stay an hour, and he told me not to worry, that his friends were on their way.

When I was saying goodbye, I didn't have the desire to kiss Scott. This didn't seem like the end of a date. I felt so cool being Scott's platonic friend—not a girl he was trying to sleep with. I felt respected by him. Scott and I were officially becoming friends, and it was a platonic divorce relationship that would teeter on a spectrum of a nonsexual thing and a passionate romance for years.

During those years, Scott dated two other friends of mine, one relationship lasting over a month, the other just a couple of weeks. As time went on, it didn't bother me so much because he was so non-committal that I knew it wouldn't work out with any of them. One time, Scott had been dating a woman named Mia for over a year and called to ask me if I wanted to come meet them for a drink. I was jealous of Mia since she was seriously drop dead gorgeous and it was the first time I'd seen Scott in love. Still, I just knew, given his track record that things with Mia would end at some point. What's notable was, I felt like she was very protective of Scott when I was around. I was deeply flattered by someone as beautiful as her seeming to feel threatened by me.

Then there was the time I met Scott's ex-wife at a party. This woman started talking about her ex-husband and when I put the pieces together, I seriously could not keep a straight face. Scott's ex was so completely different than any woman I'd ever seen him date. She was extremely intellectual and very serious. She never cracked a smile and honestly, I wasn't sure if she knew how to. What's ironic is, all Scott did was smile! He had a big grin that lit up his whole face and made you want to smile and laugh. Scott and his ex-wife were such an unlikely couple, it was bizarre. At one point during our conversation, I was trying so hard not to crack up that I had to come clean.

"Look, I'm sorry I seem like I'm about to laugh, but I know your ex-husband pretty well, and for some reason, I just think this is really funny."

She didn't ask me why I thought it was funny, and she didn't really have a strong reaction to how I was acting. Then again, she didn't have a strong reaction to anything. She was the definition of formal. She was very stoic—which was so the opposite of Scott! No wonder he was chasing every beautiful woman who walked and bailing out when things got remotely serious. He was making up for years of not having fun!

Speaking of fun. One day, Scott invited me to go on his boat and said I could bring whoever I wanted. I invited my friend, Sophia, who like me thought it was going to be the three of us. But, when we got to the pier, there were three other women going with us! That was so typical of him. A couple weeks later, I had dinner plans with Derrek, and was supposed to meet him at a restaurant at 7pm. I called him at 6:45 to tell him I was running late and would be there around 7:10. This was towards the end of our long relationship, both of us treading water to stay alive at that point, so he took my tardiness extremely offensively and started yelling at me. I had no tolerance in this stage of the game, so I shouted back, "You know what? Screw it! Let's just forget the whole thing." I hung up and who did I immediately call? You got it.

"Hi Scott, I just had a huge fight with Derrek, and I'm all dressed up and I'm hungry and really need a drink. Want to meet me for dinner?'

Scott was delighted to hear from me and told me he was in the neighborhood at Costco, buying a Robot Vacuum cleaner, and could meet in 15 minutes. I ended up having a wonderful night with him. Another bonus, at this point in my life my business was starting to grow, and who better to ask for business advice than Scott? He listened and made a lot of suggestions, many of which I ended up taking and which were successful. Then, after years of knowing Scott, it happened. Derrek and I broke up. Now I was single, and so was Scott. See, the entire time we had known each other I had been in a relationship, so there was no real pressure on either end to be anything but friends. But now the dynamic had changed. Scott seemed unfazed by it, but that was Scott—very hard to read and he was playing things casual, like he did with everyone. Through me, he had gotten to be pretty good friends with Sophia and her boyfriend. The four of us decided to go to dinner one night. There were lots of drinks (just one for me), lots of appetizers, and lots of kicks under the table from Sophia, who since meeting Scott had been dying for the two of us to end up together, minus her annoyance that he brought a harem to his boat. At the end of the night, post two or three glasses of pinot she declared, "Would the two of you just go out to the parking lot and f*cking make out already?!"

To say I wanted to die is an understatement. But the truth was, Sophia had just set the stage for an immediate deadline. If anything was ever going to happen with Scott, it had to be tonight. Right here, right now. This was the moment our entire relationship had been leading up to. We all said goodbye and when I found myself standing by my car saying goodnight to Scott, I braced myself. I knew in my heart that if Scott didn't kiss me right now, he never would.

"Well, goodnight," I said, trying not to sound nervous.

Scott hesitated and my heart was pounding. Then he leaned in. He leaned in and gave me the most platonic hug I've ever gotten in my entire life. My heart sank. It was over. My Mr. Big wasn't Mr. Big at all because he did not love me. Scott really really really liked me as a friend, but nothing else. I wasn't even upset by it. It was actually an incredible relief. I never had to wonder ever again. It was a chapter I could close. The best part was, I had a really good friend. What was so wrong with that? In the days that followed, I started to realize that just like Scott, I hadn't wanted anything more than friendship either, and that my romantic hopes were based solely on an idea and a fantasy, not the real him. If I had truly wanted to be more than friends, believe me, I'm the kind of person who would have made a move. I kept Scott in the friend zone just as much as he kept me in it. And that was just fine.

Shortly after that night, Scott sold his suburban condo and moved to the city, and we kind of lost touch. But he did show up at my 50th birthday party, and it was really good to see him.

Can Men and Women Be Friends?

I learned so much from my relationship with Scott, including the fact that men and women can be friends, especially after divorce, and that if the two of you are meant to be something more than platonic friends, it's pretty simple: one of you will make a f*cking move. I also learned that if you are in a relationship, that changes things a little bit when it comes to platonic friendships of the opposite sex. If you are in an exclusive relationship and you are going out with other men and telling yourself it's platonic, you very well could be emotionally cheating. That doesn't make you a bad person, but it does make you a cheater. Be self-aware and honest with yourself as to the motives of your platonic friendship. You owe that not only to your partner, but to yourself. Ask yourself, "How would I feel if So and So was going out with other women who were his platonic friends?" Ask yourself why you need these friendships. Is it because something is lacking in your relationship? Are you testing the waters to see if you can do better? Or is this a friend you've known since high school, college or for a very long time and it is genuinely platonic? Does this platonic friend have romantic hopes for you? I'm not saying that if you're in a romantic relationship you aren't allowed to have friends of the opposite sex. I'm just saying, be honest about what's really going on. You'll like yourself a lot more and the friendship will be so much more authentic.

CHAPTER 9

The Dalmatian
(The Denzel Washington Look-alike)

The Dalmatian is intelligent, outgoing, and beautiful. This dog turns heads wherever he goes. He certainly turned mine.

Several years ago (when I was still married to Charlie), I met a man at my gym, and we became good friends. Jordan was witty, and funny, and sharp, and he was someone I truly enjoyed running into while working out. A professional vocalist who had performed all over the country, Jordan's voice remains one of the most distinctive I've ever heard. It was remarkably deep and very low, and he had a unique and endearing laugh to go with it. Everyone who knew Jordan loved him. He was a neighborhood guy who stood out at the local bars.

Jordan had been married for a long time, and his wife, who I met only once, had passed away a couple years earlier. They had moved to my town for her career, and now Jordan, who was originally from the south, was trying to figure out his next steps. Even though he was usually the life of the party—even at the gym, where I would walk by him at times and see a circle of people standing around him enthralled by one of his sto-ries— Jordan had an underlying sadness about him that he covered up with humor and charm.

As the years went by, Jordan and I began making plans socially. The first time we met outside the gym was for lunch, and eventually, I would text him on nights when my kids were with my ex, and I felt like I needed a friend. Unlike Scott, my relationship with Jordan was always genuinely platonic. In fact, I was dating Derrek (the cheater) during much of the time I hung out with Jordan. Jordan was my sounding board when it came to relationships, especially my precarious one with Derrek. Looking back, during those Derrek years, I was seeing both Scott and Jordan. Both were platonic friends but there was a big difference in my mind. Derrek never got jealous when I went out with either guy because in his mind, they were the same.

Jordan gave great advice, and I trusted his perspective. He was brutally honest. He didn't sugarcoat anything, even things that were painful for me to hear. Whenever we talked, I always knew he was right. Did I listen to his suggestions? No, but that's my own fault. Had I taken his advice earlier, I could have saved myself years of frustration and disappointment.

So, on a Tuesday night, I texted Jordan and asked if he wanted to meet me for a drink.

"Just one drink," my message read, "I have a really busy day tomorrow. I'd just love to see you and get your advice."

What advice did I want from Jordan? Boyfriend advice, of course. I had recently ended my relationship with Derrek and was having doubts about the breakup. Obviously, I didn't know about the cheating yet.

As I sat there sipping my glass of wine, I listened to Jordan, his deep, scratchy voice making it impossible not to hear him from across the room.

"Jackie, you don't love this man," he said. "You just don't. When you realize that, it will be easier to let go."

"That's not true," I urged. "I do love him."

Jordan shook his head, "No, you don't."

It was at that moment that I saw an absolutely gorgeous man walk into the bar.

I whispered to Jordan, "See that guy? He looks like Denzel Washington."

So, what does Jordan do? He looks up, and in his Jordan voice announces, "She thinks you look like Denzel Washington."

At that moment, I wanted to crawl under the bar and not come out for a day or two. I watched Denzel break out into a dashing grin that gave me goosebumps it was so cute. He darted over to us, extended his hand to me, and declared, "I'm Chris."

I was so nervous and giggly, but I managed to introduce myself. Jordan followed suit.

"Mind if I sit with you guys?" asked Chris. "I just moved here from Minneapolis, and I don't know anyone in this town."

Chris explained that he had just gotten transferred here with his company. He was a successful corporate executive, who also happened to be a former University of Texas football player. More drinks and an hour later, the three of us were having a great time. I could tell Jordan was amused because he knew I liked this guy. What was so interesting to me was that at 47, Chris (who was a year younger than me) had never been married and didn't have any kids. He had grown up in a small town in Alabama with a single mother who he still went home to see regularly. That night, he told us he was a great son, but wasn't sure what kind of husband he would be. He explained that he had been engaged once, but that it didn't pan out. I couldn't believe it. No woman had been able to grab this great guy?!

A few minutes later, Jordan got a text from a mutual acquaintance telling him she was at a karaoke bar down the street and that we should come. So, the three of us walked down there and spent the next couple hours talking, laughing, and singing along to Whitney Houston, Lionel Richie, Elvis, and Madonna with our fellow drunk neighbors, including our friend, Alexis, who has a gift for rap. Yes, it's true. Five foot two, 100 pounds and blond and she could compete with Eminem. It wasn't until I looked at my phone and saw that it was 1:04 a.m., that I realized I needed to get home, so I ordered an Uber.

Chris walked me to the doorway of the bar and while he waited for my ride with me, asked me out for dinner. How interesting that I had started off the night considering getting back together with Derrek, only to be talked out of it by Jordan, and now I already had a date. A gorgeous date!

"How about Saturday?" he asked.

Inside, I was jumping up and down. "That will work."

We exchanged numbers and hugged, and I got into the Uber one happy camper.

Chris texted me the next day, telling me that he enjoyed meeting me, and that he was looking forward to our date. He told me he was looking for a gym to join (which made sense since his body was seriously perfect: athletic, muscular, toned, and hard) so I suggested the gym where Jordan and I went. I also told him I was taking a kickboxing class the next morning and that he should try it out.

"Sounds great!" he said, "What time? I'll be there."

Now, you have to understand that the kickboxing class was being taught by my friend, Katy, the best fitness instructor on earth, but nonetheless a then 55-year-old with a clientele of women in their 40s and up. So, I was a little nervous to see how this group of women would react when they saw Chris.

I got there first, and sure enough, when Chris walked in, the entire room stared at him. I found it hilarious, and even funnier when I introduced him to Katy right before the class, knowing that now everyone knew he was with me. Confidently, Chris put his mat in the front row and started stretching and warming up with some punches. I was trying not to laugh at the expressions on these women's faces, oohing and ahhhing over him. I was also focused on the fact that Chris was seeing me in workout clothes with no makeup. Would he still want to have dinner with me, or would he realize he had beer goggles on the other night? I managed to make it through the class, although I did what every single woman in the class did for the entire hour—stare at Chris. Actually, it made the class go by really fast! Chris said he liked the class, but never went back. He would later tell me he attended just to see me, which was adorable.

Saturday night came, and since Chris was new in town, it was up to me to pick the restaurant. He pulled up to my house in his Lexus two-seater convertible and walked up to the door. I gave him a quick tour of the first floor and off we went to an intimate Italian restaurant in the next town over. We walked in and that's when something happened that I had never experienced before: People were staring at us. This was not in my head. Every person at every single table seemed to have their eyeballs on us. It was uncomfortable. Why the stares? Maybe because they thought Chris was a famous athlete? Maybe because he was so handsome? Or maybe it was because a white girl and a black guy were out together. It was as if I suddenly woke up from a race coma I'd been living in my entire life. It was almost surreal, and I was having a hard time even focusing because I couldn't believe the sight of us together was drawing so much attention. We were just another couple on a date. What was different about us? Color. Period. I was absolutely disgusted, especially when I saw a woman I knew through business having dinner with who I surmised was her husband.

As I was walking by, I smiled and said, "Hi, Emily!"

The look she gave me was one I will seriously never forget. I interpreted it as her asking me, "Why are you with a black man?" I felt judged.

I had never experienced this while being out with Jordan, who is also black. I never sensed anyone was staring at us or judging us as an interracial couple. What was the difference? Maybe that Jordan and I were always in our own neighborhood where everyone knew us? Maybe I just never noticed? I also didn't feel judged by any of the women in the fitness class when Chris was there. I will say this: the 30-second walk Chris and I took from the hostess stand to our table changed my view of racism forever.

We sat down and I looked at Chris and asked, "Why is everyone staring?"

"Ummm…because I'm black?"

He didn't say it in a mean way, he sort of laughed when he said it.

"Chris, I am so sorry. I had no idea people would act this way."
"It's not your fault. Really," he replied.

"You know, Chris, I've never been on a date with a black man."

Chris laughed. "I can see that."

After that, we dropped it, and I have to say, we ended up having a lovely dinner, with the exception that every time I looked around the restaurant, I could see people looking at us. During dinner, I asked Chris why at 47 he was still single and had never married. He talked about being raised by a single mom but wasn't willing to open up about it.

"Do you want kids?" I asked.

"Not sure about that one yet, but I do love kids," he replied.

I couldn't decide if Chris's responses were immature, or a way to ditch any kind of serious conversation on this topic. I wanted to ask if he was in therapy but didn't. Chris asked me a lot of questions about my kids, and I showed him some pics on my phone. His smile and comments were really cute. After dinner, Chris drove me home and walked me to my door.

"I'm not going to come in, but I just want to tell you I had a great time tonight," he said.

"I did, too," I smiled. Then I got really nervous because I knew Chris was about to lean in for a kiss.

"Is this OK?" he whispered, as he began leaning.

I didn't answer, but I kissed him back for a minute. Looking back, Chris's kiss was wonderful. It was soft and gentle and sweet and sexy, but because of my recent breakup, I wasn't in a place to enjoy it. I felt guilty, like I was cheating on Derrek. Ironic, isn't it? When it comes to Chris, I always say, "What a waste. Worst timing ever." I truly think if I met Chris at a different time, things could have turned out differently.

This isn't the ending I know you want, but I ended the relationship with Chris and got back together with Derrek. It would be the first of about four or five breakups before our last breakup. When Derrek and I were finally done, I got in touch with Chris, and he didn't seem interested anymore. I think he was seeing someone. I will always have really warm, wonderful memories of Chris, and feel like whoever he ended up with is one lucky woman. I have no idea where he is today, but I was in an Uber in Florida a few years ago, and the driver told me where he worked, and it was the same company Chris worked for. So, I took a chance and asked him, "Do you know Chris So and So?"

"I know Chris," he said enthusiastically. "Great guy."

I told him I agreed and smiled.

My Thoughts on Racism

I realize now that until my date with Chris, I was naïve about racism. It's not that I didn't care, I had just never witnessed it firsthand. What happened to us in that restaurant changed my rosy picture of America and awakened me to the realities of prejudice, judgment, and discrimination. And now, I am one more person who can fight for less racism and more unity, less bigotry and more open-mindedness, and less hatred and more love.

What to Consider When Dating a Guy Who Has Never Been Married and Has No Children

1. Kids.

I've found that a divorced guy who has kids has a certain ease around children, which can make getting to know your children a little easier. Of course, there are always exceptions. The thing is, if you are dating someone who hasn't been around kids much, they might not enjoy being around yours. It might be awkward at first. Or it might turn out great. I have a feeling it would have been wonderful with Chris.

2. The ability to be domestic. In other words, can he play house?

Let's face it. Once you've been married, you've seen it all and smelled it all, from annoying habits (leaving clothes all over the floor) to bodily functions (burping and farting). Can a guy who has never been married handle this? Maybe, maybe not. Maybe he's lived with someone, or maybe he'll run for the hills the first time he sees you sitting on the bathtub ledge clipping your toenails. Then again, maybe I'm not giving the guy who has never been married enough credit. Maybe love and commitment can overcome all those things.

3. Baggage.

Here's a plus for the guy who has never been married: He's carrying way less baggage than the divorced guy. He's not bashing his ex every three days, he's not saying good-bye to his kids and then having that sad look on his face, and he doesn't have that wounded look that says, "My wife ruined my life." The man who has never been married is fresh, untainted, perhaps. Although, how do I know he wasn't madly in love and then dumped? Is his breakup any less significant because he wasn't legally married? Everyone has baggage, but the divorced man's baggage tends to be a little heavier, given kids, legal issues, assets, finances, and more.

4. Commitment.

Perhaps the biggest factor in dating a man who has never been married: there's commitment and then there's commitment. The divorced guy committed. He stood in front of God or a judge and a crowd of people and agreed to commit. He also signed a legal document. A man who has never been married could have a commitment issue. Again, I'm not bashing Chris or any other man who has never been married. I don't know the story.

He could have always wanted to commit and just never found the right person, or maybe he committed (got engaged) and then the girl broke it off. Who knows. All I'm saying is, the divorced guy proved he had the willingness to be completely and utterly monogamous. (Then again, he could have been a huge cheater in the marriage.) Plus, maybe he never wants to commit again.

The bottom line is, both a divorced man and a man who has never been married can be amazing guys. They can also both be jerks. In other words, one is not better than the other. It's not easy but try not to define someone based on whether or not they have ever been married.

Everyone has a different story and a reason why they ended up divorced or never married. Maybe it's by choice, maybe it's bad luck (or good luck), and maybe it shouldn't even be factored into the relationship. In other words, maybe it doesn't even matter. What does matter? The individual person. Is he going to love you unconditionally? Will he be here for you if you really need him? Can you trust him? Is he your best friend? Those are a lot more important questions than "Has he ever been married?"

CHAPTER 10

The Labradoodle
(The Lesbian)

The Labradoodle is affectionate, playful, and kindhearted. This dog loves being loved. In a way, I loved her.

How am I a local star?" I asked my friend, Audrey, who was seated next to me, the two of us watching our sons' travel basketball practice.

"You are a Chicago Tribune columnist," she said. "Believe me, you are a great fit for this. Please, Jackie?! I'm desperate."

Audrey was organizing a local "Dancing with the Stars" competition to raise money for a lovely organization that subsidized our kids' public schools. Twelve local "stars," including a junior high school principal, a veteran police officer, and a state senator, were being matched up with a professional dance instructor and would compete in a one-night event in front of an audience of 400 community members and one judge. I really was flattered to have been asked but was also apprehensive since I am seriously a terrible dancer. I have two sisters who are both amazing dancers. Either one of them would have jumped at the chance to partici-pate in this, but one is a doctor and the other works in commercial real estate, and neither live in my community. At the time, I was also in need of a hip replacement and walked with a slight limp. How was I going to dance when I couldn't even walk normally? Audrey kept telling me how tough I was, and how I shouldn't use my hip as an excuse when she sees me at the gym five days a week.

Two or three basketball practices later, I committed. This meant practicing once a week for six months with my 21-year-old professional dance instructor, who would be my partner in the competition. The dance studio was thirty minutes away and in addition to the one-on-one ses-sions, there were group practices every couple of weeks. All the couples had to learn the ensemble dances that would open and close the show.

During a group practice, I met Veronica, a really pretty forty-some-thing woman, whose eyes were big and beautiful, and whose love and pas-sion for life were even bigger and more beautiful. I clicked with Veronica from day one, and we became friends. I loved her energy. I loved that she had two or three jobs and still found time to volunteer, and I loved her full figure, her Spanish accent, her love of peach gelato, and her giggle. But beneath all her positivity and enthusiasm, Veronica was very sad; heart-broken, actually. Her wife of three years had just broken up with her.

Naturally, since I wrote and still write articles giving relationship advice, I took Veronica under my wing and began coaching her. I listened, counseled her, pumped her up, and assured her she would have no prob-lem meeting someone else. It was around the second or third month of knowing each other that I started to sense that Veronica, massively on the rebound, had developed romantic feelings for me. She was always compli-menting the way I looked, and I caught her staring at me a few times. She was flirty with me, but in a non-intrusive way. The funny part was, I kind of liked the attention and I liked her, so I started thinking about what it would be like to date her. Could I kiss her? Possibly. Could I sleep with her? Highly doubtful.

One night, I was walking out of practice when Veronica called my name. I turned around and she ran over to me in the parking lot.

"Hey, what are you up to Saturday night?" she asked. "Would you want to go out to dinner with me?"

I looked around to see if anyone heard. This is how rumors start. I then thought about how nice it was that she was direct and to the point, and she was asking me out for a Saturday night date, and it was only Monday. None of the other dogs did that. I made a decision right then that I could go on the date and decide during dinner if I wanted anything more than friendship. But just to play it safe, my answer was completely honest.

"I would love to go out with you Saturday, but I have to be upfront with you. I really like you. I think you're so pretty and if I was gay, I would be really interested. But I'm not gay. So, if you want to go out with me, I'd love to go out, but you need to know that the dinner is nothing more than platonic."

She stood there thoughtful for a second and then said, "Sure! Sounds like a plan." Then she kissed my cheek and ran off. It felt kind of whimsical and I was really happy and looking forward to Saturday night. Whatever was going to happen (or not happen) was a win-win. Who knows? Maybe I was done with male dogs. Maybe a girlfriend was what I needed at this point in my life. It all sounded very cool, with one exception: imagining myself in bed with a woman just didn't do it for me. But I loved Veronica as a friend, so if she was OK with us being platonic friends, great.

What would happen over the next few days changed everything. Veronica began texting me that Monday night after I got home and didn't stop for three days. The texts came frequently and were long and romantic. She was spilling her heart out. It was as if she hadn't listened to anything I said and was now trying to convince me to have a romantic relationship with her.

"You have the cutest smile." "I dream of you when I fall asleep and when I wake up." "We are so alike, we are aligned." Stuff like that.

It went on and on, and I was having anxiety every time I heard the bling on my phone. By Thursday, I had to call Veronica and tell her the date was off.

"I really like you, but I told you that I just wanted to be friends and you aren't respecting how I feel," I told her.

Her response was cold and unemotional. "OK, no big deal."

"See you at practice?" I asked.

"Sure."

The next few weeks seeing Veronica were stressful for me because she wouldn't talk to me or even look at me. I wasn't sure if she was embarrassed or mad at me for rejecting her. Had I led her on? I started to feel guilty, like I had done something wrong befriending Veronica.

The night of the show, I had other things on my mind besides a scorned Veronica, like performing in my 49-year-old body in front of 400 community members! It was terrifying and surreal, but I did it. My heart was pounding the entire three minutes I was on stage, and in the end, I felt very proud of myself for the guts it took to perform, and for raising the money I did for my kids' schools. As I was leaving the event, I ran into Veronica, and we said good-bye to each other, but it was very awkward.

A couple weeks after the show, the sponsors held a cast party to thank us for our time and hard work. A lot of people brought spouses. I did not. Surprisingly enough, Veronica brought a date. I tried to say hello, but she turned away. I caught her and her friend staring at me a couple times, and at this point, their behavior felt very uncomfortable and to be honest, immature. Nothing had happened between us! I wasn't Veronica's ex-lover, so why was she acting like I was? Perhaps the worst part of the evening was when one of the dancers—a legendary librarian who I found to be stuffy and judgmental, came over to the cocktail table where I was standing and grabbed a jacket off one of the chairs.

"This is Veronica's," she said in a pretty bitchy tone. "She asked me to come get it and bring it to her."

Now I was pissed. God only knows what Veronica was telling people. Did people in my community think I dated and dumped Veronica?! It really didn't seem fair, and I didn't want or deserve to get a negative reputation. I left the party shortly after, only to glance back one last time and see Veronica and her date, both giving me a dirty look. To this day, I don't really understand what I did wrong. Did I lead Veronica on? Was I a tease? Not at all. I can always hang my hat on the fact that I was honest and upfront with this woman. For that, I'm proud of myself.

The Benefits of Honesty in a Relationship

I learned two things from my "relationship" with Veronica. One, I know 100% that I am not gay. I was curious for about two minutes, and I had every right to explore those feelings. But that was the extent of it. Second, being honest was the right thing to do. If there is any chance you think someone is interested in you, and you don't have those same feelings, being honest and open right from the start is the way to go. Not only is it fair to the other person, but you're doing yourself a favor.

Here are 16 dishonest things people say in relationships, and what I WISH the person would say instead.

1. I just don't want a girlfriend right now.

Honest version: I don't want you to be my girlfriend. It's nothing personal. You're a really good person, but this just doesn't feel right for me. I'm so sorry. I don't want to hurt you.

2. I'm sort of seeing someone right now.

Honest version: I have a girlfriend but I'm not sure she's the one. Otherwise, I wouldn't have gone out with you in the first place. Going out with you made me realize I want to be with her. I'm sorry. I didn't mean to hurt you.

3. It's not you, it's me.

Honest version: It's you. I just don't see this going anywhere. I'm sorry. I don't want to hurt you.

4. I want to date other people.

Honest version: I want to see if I can meet someone I like better because I'm not sure about this relationship, but I don't want to risk losing you.

5. I just want to have fun.

Honest version: I don't want to be exclusive because I'm not sure you are the one yet. I am also enjoying the sex.

6. This really isn't working out.

Honest version: I'm breaking up with you.

7. You're a great guy. I don't deserve you.

Honest version: I don't want to be with you anymore and I feel guilty because you're a really good person.

8. What are you doing right now? (over the phone)

Honest version: Want me to come over and have sex with you?

9. I don't like myself right now.

Honest version: If I saw a future with you, I would make changes and be my best self because I would never want to lose you.

10. You're going to make some guy really, really happy.

Honest version: You're not making me happy.

11. I don't want to fight anymore.

Honest version: I wish we could go back to the first 6 months of our relationship when we were on our best behavior, because we both know this is going downhill fast.

12. Sorry I haven't called. I've been so busy with work.

Honest version: I met someone else and dated her for a couple weeks and it just ended. Or I wasn't really into you and then I changed my mind.

13. *I'm just happy with the way things are.*

Honest version: I don't want to marry you.

14. *I'm going out of town. I'll call you when I get back.*

Honest version: I'm not into you, because if I was, it doesn't matter where I am. I'd call or even text or email or snapchat. This is 2024.

15. *I don't have time for a relationship right now.*

Honest version: I don't want to be in a relationship with you.

16. *I'm really confused. I don't know what I want.*

Honest version: I might be confused, but I'm not confused about the fact that I know I don't want to be with you.

Here's the thing. Brutal honesty might really really hurt. It might break your heart. It might make you cry. But wouldn't you rather know the truth than cling onto hope that the person might change their mind in a few days or weeks? That is the benefit of honesty in a relationship. Don't we all deserve honesty? Hearing the truth, despite the pain it causes, helps people move on. Remember, there is a nice way to say everything. You can still be honest and be kind.

CHAPTER 11

The Goldendoodle
(The Hot Baseball Coach)

The Goldendoodle is friendly and loving, and even though this dog is full of energy, he has a calm demeanor. I love this dog so much.

If someone asked me what you need for a happy, healthy, and fulfilling romantic relationship, my answer would be these things (in no particular order): good communication, emotional and physical attraction, fun, genuine friendship, good sex, likability, trust, loyalty, respect, and authenticity. But there's one thing I feel that might be the most important factor which makes a relationship over-the-top wonderful and long lasting: The person brings out the best in you. What I mean by this is that his love and presence in your life is like a powerful drug that gives you strength, confidence, and drive to be the best person you can be in every aspect of your life. That deep happiness from the relationship bleeds into your desire to give back to others. This can come in the form of doing volunteer work, being more motivated at work, being a better parent, being a better friend, or acting in thoughtful, giving ways to other people. It's almost like receiving a magical cape with superpowers. You had it in you, you just needed someone to help bring it out. That's what Tom did for me.

I had been divorced for about a year or two when my ex-husband insisted we sign our second-grade son up for park district baseball. Rolling my eyes thinking about how every dad feels the need for his son to play sports, I obliged. The first day of practice was the first time I ever saw Tom: a really nice-looking Irish guy with an athletic build and pretty blue eyes. But Tom got even more attractive when I started watching the way he interacted with my son and the other team members. It was adorable. He treated them like little boys but at the same time, he maintained a firmness and a command for respect. Looking back, I think I fell in love with Tom the first day I saw him. But let me make something very clear. Tom was married at the time, and I assumed happily. He had three kids, one of whom was on the team. So, I'm not saying I was trying to date Tom or trying to get him to cheat on his wife. It was a harmless crush, and actually, I think every mom whose kid was on the team felt the same way I did. What's funny is, I probably had one or two conversations with him the entire season, one being the day of the last game when I handed him a $25 Dick's gift card to say thank you.

A few years would go by before I saw Tom again. It was at a junior high school basketball game where our boys' school teams were playing each other. Tom was sitting in the stands with one of his daughters. We said hello and that was it. Over the next couple years, I would run into Tom at travel basketball games, team tryouts, and other sports related events. One time, at a travel basketball practice, I introduced Tom to Derrek. I remember thinking that Tom seemed a little territorial, like he was my big brother, and he seemed a little skeptical.

"How long have you been dating Derrek?" he asked me.

"A long time."

"How's that going?" he asked.

I found it strange (and a little bit exciting) that he was interested in knowing that information. After that night, a year would go by until I ran into Tom again. One day, I was picking up my son from a different travel basketball tryout, and something strange happened. I remember clearly that when Tom and I smiled and waved from a distance, I was thinking, "He looks pretty happy to see me." My gut told me right then that Tom was either getting divorced or that he was divorced. I was getting such a different vibe than I'd always gotten in the past. That said, I had no proof and didn't see Tom again for at least another year.

When you belong to the same gym for a decade, you pretty much know everyone there—both the employees and the members. It's a really nice feeling, and it's comforting and fun to see the same people day in and day out. Remember Jordan? I saw him at the gym daily. The problem with knowing so many people at the gym is, by the time you're done talking to everyone, what should have been a 45-minute workout turns into two hours. So, one day while at the gym, I walked over to the area where the exercise machines are located, and who do I spot doing the elliptical? Tom! I found myself delighted to see him. It had now been about five years since he coached my son.

"Hi Coach Tom!" I exclaimed with the energy of a high-school cheerleader. "Do you remember me?"

"Of course," he said.

He asked about my son, and we had the catch-up conversation. Tom told me he had just joined the gym. Seeing him set the tone for a wonderful workout and day ahead. There was something about Tom that put me in a happy mood. It had always been that way. He emitted positivity and warmth, and at the same time an intense drive and motivation that felt contagious. I assumed Tom was still married, despite the one time I felt like his face lit up like a Christmas tree when he saw me, but I confirmed it by doing the wedding ring glance, and yep, that gold band was still on his left ring finger. Darn it! But remember, I was still in a long-term relationship with Derrek.

A couple days went by and when I walked into the gym, there was Tom, once again on the elliptical. I didn't hesitate. I walked up and got on the machine next to his.

"Hi," I said. "Do you mind?"

"Of course not."

Thirty minutes on the elliptical went by amazingly fast since Tom and I talked non-stop the entire time. This time our conversation was about work—his career and my business—I had recently started Divorced Girl Smiling. It was also during this time that I was looking for a full-time job. Tom gave great advice, almost like a career coach. When I finished working out, I felt so inspired, like I could accomplish anything. Over the next few weeks, I'd see Tom at the gym almost daily. Sometimes I'd work out next to him and other times we would just wave or say a quick hello. I never felt like our relationship was inappropriate because it wasn't flirtatious. It was genuine. We had a connection, which was built on likeability and respect. It wasn't romantic. And just for the record, I had many other married male friends at the gym, and there was nothing going on with any of them. I also had many female friends at the gym. It was the culture there. So many friendships were formed between women, men, and members of the opposite sex. It was actually really lovely. So, Tom was a part of that.

One morning, after a huge fight with Derrek the night before (the same night I met Scott out for dinner), I walked into the gym, saw Tom on an elliptical, and darted over.

"Thank God you're here!" I exclaimed as if he was my best girlfriend.

"What's up?" he asked.

I got on the machine and started telling him about the fight, how I was unsure of my relationship, how I'd had dinner with Scott, how I felt like an emotional cheater, and how unhappy I was.

"We've been together for so long that I honestly just don't know how to get out of it."

Tom appeared to consider his response thoughtfully, but when he finally gave his advice, he spoke with authority.

"I say you've got to get rid of this guy."

That made me chuckle because it was so blunt. I loved how honest and real and non-sugarcoated he was. I also knew he was right. But did I listen? Nope. Several months went by, and I was still talking to Tom a few times a week at the gym. When I'd walk in and see him, I'd feel so happy. He was becoming a friend I truly enjoyed and someone I looked up to. Tom was a little bit like Scott in that I respected him, got advice from him, and really liked being around him, but the two men and the two relationships were entirely different. With Scott, there was always an underlying flirtation, a possibility of turning the friendship into romance. With Tom, a married man, I never considered it and neither did he. Tom was like my own personal coach, and he gave me really good advice on many, many things. I'd acted on a lot of his suggestions, except for the breakup with Derrek. I was still hanging on, hoping we could work things out. I did truly care for Derrek.

On Valentine's Day, Derrek and I broke up for what would be the last time. This time there was no going back. When your boyfriend calls you the C word (Also known as: C U Next Tuesday), I'd say it's time to end the relationship. Yes, I was called the C word on Valentine's Day. How do you come back from that? You don't. The good news about being called the C word is that you aren't even sad about the breakup because all you have to keep saying to yourself is, 'This guy called me the C word.' Done. The End. Finished. The other good news about being called the C word, especially on Valentine's Day is that Valentine's Day in the future can never be worse than that Valentine's Day. Derrek set the bar so low that it's laughable.

When I walked into the gym the next morning and saw Tom on the elliptical, I debated whether to even work out next to him because I didn't want to tell him about the name calling. It was so humiliating. Then again, I needed a friend and he had become a really good one.

"Hi…" I said as I got on the machine next to his.

"Uh oh…What's wrong?" he asked.

"Well, we broke up, and this time it's for good."

"Are you OK?"

"Yes," I said. "I know I did the right thing."

Tom talked me through it that day, and again the next day, and every time I saw him over the next few weeks. The next couple of months, I spent a lot of time alone. I was very relieved to be out of a situation I had known in my heart for a very long time was wrong. During those weeks, I went out to dinners with girlfriends, met Jordan for drinks a few times, spent a lot of time with my kids, engaged in more therapy, and rehearsed for the upcoming "Dancing with the Local Stars." (Things with Veronica had already ended.) It was also during this time that I got closure with Scott at our dinner with Sophia and her husband.

I had been broken up with Derrek for about two months when I was working on a feature story for the Chicago Tribune about a new spa treatment called "floating," also known as Restricted Environment Stimulation Therapy (REST). While interviewing Frank, a local wellness spa owner, we realized we had a mutual friend. That night, the mutual friend called me and insisted that Frank and I go out on a date. Reluctant, but truly wanting to get that first date after a long-term relationship out of the way, I agreed. Frank called and we made plans for Friday night.

A few days before the date, I told Tom about it while we were working out.

His response was unconvincing. "OK, well that's good I guess."

An awkward silence followed.

"Do you think I shouldn't go?" I asked. "Are you thinking I'm not ready?"

"No, I didn't say that," he said. "Hey, can I tell you something?"

"Sure," I replied. I had no idea about the bomb Tom was about to drop.

"I'm getting divorced."

Hearing these words were truly shocking. I honestly had no clue. My head started to spin. I mean, all this time my impression had been that things in Tom's marriage were good, that he would be married until the day he died. One, Tom is Catholic. They don't take divorce lightly. In fact, they just don't divorce period. Secondly, Tom had always talked so lovingly about his three children and all the time they spent together, that I felt like he'd never want to live apart from them. And third, in the past year and a half I'd been talking to him, he'd been nothing but positive, upbeat, and genial—not the personality traits of someone going through a divorce. Turns out, Tom had been having problems for the past few years and had been trying to work things out. He had recently realized that wasn't going to happen, and that he didn't have a choice. Divorce was imminent.

After the initial shock, things started to make sense to me. I was the type of person who made friends with everyone at the gym, whereas Tom was/is a pretty private guy. He didn't socialize around the gym like I did. He had probably fostered a friendship with me to try to soothe his pain and loneliness. After all, I was a Chicago Tribune relationship columnist. Looking back, maybe I subconsciously knew deep down that Tom didn't have a good marriage, and maybe I had ulterior motives the whole time. But consciously, I had no clue. But there was something else. Suddenly I felt like complete crap for not being there for him. He had listened to my relationship problems, he had coached me career-wise, he had motivated me and inspired me, and what had I brought to the table? Then again, he chose not to share anything with me. I felt a bit betrayed by that, but I understood. I think Tom waited to tell me until he was absolutely sure his marriage was over. And I think he was trying to save it the entire time.

I was still trying to swim in all the emotions I was feeling when one grabbed me. Hard. Tom was single and I was elated. Guilt followed. He was going through the pain of a divorce and secretly, part of me felt like running into the locker room and doing cartwheels. We talked about his impending divorce for a little while, and when I was done with my workout, I started getting off the machine. That's when Tom asked me to lunch.

"Listen…forget lunch," I declared. "We need to go out for cocktails."

My weekend plans were shaping up like this: Friday night, date with Frank, Saturday night, I didn't know what to call it with Tom. On Friday, I went to get my nails done and bought a new pair of sandals, and as I was handing my credit card over to the cashier at DSW, I realized I was doing all of this for my gym buddy, not Frank. Friday afternoon, when I still hadn't heard from Frank (red flag, by the way), I texted him.

"Still on for tonight?"

The text back was shocking. "My buddy's aunt died, and I have to go over to his house and be with him."

To say I was pissed is putting it mildly. This was just plain old bad dating behavior, in my opinion. First off, I had just written an article for the Chicago Tribune that made Frank's business glow. The lack of gratitude was disturbing. Secondly, was he even going to text me to cancel the date? I was actually relieved that I didn't have to go, but still, I wasn't happy with Frankie boy's treatment of me. What a complete wimp. If he changed his mind, all he had to do was text and cancel the day before. And, if his excuse was legit, all he had to do was text and cancel when he found out. The fact that he didn't mention rescheduling told me there was no dead aunt.

The good news was, I quickly forgot about Frank the second I got into Tom's car on Saturday night. He looked great. So different from the gym—all cleaned up and really, really handsome. We decided to go to a restaurant that was a couple towns away so we wouldn't see anyone we knew. We ordered drinks, ate guacamole and chips, and just talked and talked non-stop. It all felt very comfortable, like we had such a great head start from talking on the ellipticals for the past two years. What was so nice is that we weren't rushed. Being with Tom was very relaxing. To this day, I still say that being around Tom is like taking Xanax. He has such a calming effect on me because he is so peaceful by nature. After dinner, I invited Tom into my house, and we talked for about another hour, him sitting on the couch, me sitting on the carpet in front of the fireplace. When he was leaving, we kissed on the lips, but it was close-mouthed, so it technically could have been platonic, but we both knew it wasn't. The next day, I got a really nice text from him, and that is how my current nine-year relationship with the hot baseball coach began.

Tom is the person I think and hope is my last love (simply because I hope I'm still with him when I die or vice versa.) There have been so many firsts with Tom. He's the first person who truly gets and accepts me for who

I am. He's the first person I get and who I accept for who he is. He's the first person who's ever treated me with the love and affection I realize I actually deserve. He's the first person I feel I can truly be myself with and he still loves me, despite my many flaws. Tom is the first person I've ever traveled extensively with. He's the first person who has ever bought me nice jewelry, including a beautiful ring I wear on my left ring finger as a symbol of our eternal commitment. We might get married, but there's no rush.

The biggest first with Tom is the clarity I have when it comes to knowing I'm with the right person. In every other relationship—even my marriage—I always had doubts. I thought that was normal, and maybe it is, even for those in a happy, healthy romantic relationship. But for me, looking back, I always had one foot out the door, one eye on the guy two barstools over from me, and half my heart unwilling to fully devote it to anyone. I'm not saying I was a cheater in my relationships, but rather that in retrospect, I now know I was cheating myself. Because of fear or not liking myself or bad timing, I wasn't all-in like I am now.

I'm not going to tell you that Tom is perfect or that our relationship is perfect every minute of every day. Perfection does not exist. We all have flaws. Some are endearing, some annoying, and some you just want to scream your head off in frustration and throw something! But to accept faults and weaknesses in a person and continue to love him or her is true commitment. It's our flaws that make us human, and theoretically, being with a perfect person would get tedious and dull. In a happy, healthy relationship, to be angry or disappointed or frustrated by your spouse, at times, is normal. It's called unconditional love, and when you're both aware of your staying power, it only makes the relationship stronger and richer.

Here are the things that make this relationship work:

1. Tom brings out the best in me.

I think people show up a little bit differently in every relationship. For example, I truly loved Charlie, my ex-husband, but I didn't like the person I was when I was with him. I was mean, at times, angry, impatient, and selfish. That's not me. That's not entirely Charlie's fault, by the way. I take ownership of who I was back then, a new mother who was frustrated in my career and who felt guilty for not enjoying being a stay-at-home mom. Had I had the self-awareness back then that I do today, I would have been a better partner in marriage. In my relationship with Brad, the hot and cold guy, it seemed no matter how hard I tried, I always felt insecure and like I was chasing him, which is terrible for self-esteem. When I was with Noah, the too nice guy, I didn't like myself enough to feel I deserved his love, probably because I wasn't even close to being at peace with my divorce. And with Drew, the addict, without even realizing it, he bulldozed my self-esteem to the ground because who would stay in such an abusive relationship, even for a week? A person whose self-esteem was flattened like a pancake.

The thing about Tom is that from day one, I have really liked how I present as a person with him. Tom doesn't get all the credit. I think a lot of why it works is that I've done the work—the therapy, the self-reflection, the forgiveness of myself, and the building of a professional life based on what I love to do: write, broadcast and help others. That brings me joy, but it also brings me self-love and self-pride. I'm also more patient, I don't fly off the handle at little things, I have a lot more gratitude than I used to, and I'm proud of the way I've raised my children. However, Tom does play a big role in me liking myself, as well. He's made it easy because he's the kind of person who will use his love to build you up, give you strength and confidence, get you through the tough times, and make you feel like you can do anything. Tom is the best life coach I've ever had. He makes me want to be the best person I can be, and the way he treats me has taught me how to treat others, how to be a better parent, and how to be a really good partner.

2. *Utter trust and commitment.*

About four years into our relationship, I shattered my wrist, was rushed to the hospital, and had to have surgery that day to insert a plate and nine screws into my arm. During the months of healing and recovering that followed, Tom came over almost every night with dinner for my kids and me. He did laundry and dishes, walked the dog, and sat on the couch with me, scratched my back, and watched movies with me for hours.

Several months later, I was diagnosed with thyroid cancer and had to have another surgery. Again, he showed up for me. I will never, ever forget his commitment and loyalty to me. It means the world. People always ask me if I'm ever going to get married again, but the truth is, what I have runs as deep, if not deeper than some marriages. Love is a choice, and Tom and I have an understanding that we are here for each other in every possible way. It's something I am grateful for every day because there is no better gift than that.

3. The two of us are our best selves.

One time I told Tom I found it hard to believe he ended up divorced. "I mean, who would ever divorce you?" I asked. Tom explained that he was not the husband or the man back then that he is today. Tom said he spent a few years in weekly therapy and made some life changes to better himself. He told me that I am actually getting the best of him. It made me realize that he is also getting my best self. With every relationship and in aging, in general, I believe people keep evolving and growing, hopefully for the better. So even though aging can be really challenging, especially physically, there are benefits to getting older and loving at an older age.

4. Tom's hot.

Sex, rather good sex, is important to most people. It's not the most important thing, but there's something about good sex that keeps a couple connected emotionally and in a romantic space. Sex is most important to a couple at the beginning of a relationship, when everything is fresh and new, and you just can't get enough of the person. But over time, the physical part becomes less important, with trust, loyalty, likability, respect, and commitment keeping the two people together instead of the heart-stopping feeling you get in bed. That said, sex is still important, and sex will always be important. How do you keep the romance alive?

Coming from someone who is still madly in love after nine years, and someone whose heart still melts at the sight of her boyfriend, I can tell you that yes, there is work involved in keeping the fire hot. But the work should be work that both people want to do, not work they feel obligated or stressed about doing. What I mean by "work" is making dinner reservations on Saturday nights, writing your spouse a cute message on a Post-it (I have dozens of these saved from Tom and he does, too, from me), planning weekend getaways, giving your spouse a backrub without them asking, doing the dishes after dinner one night and telling your spouse "I got this," buying your spouse flowers for no reason, helping your spouse role play for a job interview, watching the show your spouse wants to watch, hosting your mother-in-law for a month and not complaining about it, or even just asking your spouse to go for a walk with you, just because you missed him or her today and you want to catch up. These kind and thoughtful gestures are foreplay to great sex.

Think about it. When you feel gratitude for your spouse and all he/she does for you, you feel such immense love for them that you are happy to express that love. On the flip side, who wants to have sex with someone who is mean to them or who doesn't speak to them with respect or who blows off their birthday? Get the picture?

5. We're best friends.

This one sounds a little trite, but nothing is truer. In all my relationships, I'm not sure if I was ever friends with the guys. I saw them as romantic partners, and failed to see the importance of being real, genuine friends and partners. A friend will do anything for you. A friend will be honest with you. A friend will support you when you're doing well versus get competitive and jealous. A friend will be there for you when you are grieving a death or something else. And a friend won't judge you. I knew Tom and I were best friends very early on, but that concept really hit home when I broke my wrist and couldn't drive. I had scheduled a job interview which was an hour and a half from my house. Tom told me not to cancel it, and that he would drive me and wait for me, which he did. I think it's a lot easier to fall in love than to find someone you truly like as a person. People say I love you all the time. They have a hard time saying I'm sorry, and they almost never say I really like you.

6. We laugh a lot.

My love of men who make me laugh dates back to the day I was born. I had a very funny dad, whose humorous personality was adored by everyone who knew him. So, growing up, I assumed that all men were funny, and that women and the kids were supposed to just sit there and laugh and be entertained by the husband's humor.

My dad's friends were really funny, too, so the first time I realized that not all men were funny, I was very confused. I was probably 6 years old at the time, and I was at a friend's house. The girl's dad came home from work. I watched him, and I kept waiting for the punch line. Seriously. I could not believe he wasn't being funny. It seemed odd to me how serious he was. So, because of my experiences, when I grew up, I was always attracted to men who made me laugh. I have been in relationships with men who weren't particularly good looking, who didn't have the best bodies, and who weren't the sharpest tools in the shed, but who I enjoyed immensely because of their wit and ability to make me laugh until my cheeks hurt.

First of all, joking around and laughing are great icebreakers for a first date that can otherwise be uncomfortable and awkward. Second, have you ever seen a person laughing and thought that person looked unattractive? Never! People who are happy, giddy, laughing, and smiling look good! So, if your guy is funny, he will be laughing at his own jokes, and you will be laughing, and you will look better to each other.

Another great thing is that laughing just feels good inside. It's nice to temporarily forget about our problems and the problems of the world, or even more so, to make fun of our problems. If something bad is going on in your life, why not joke about it at times? Humor is a wonderful healer and great for the soul. Here's a great example. Remember that movie, Crazy, Stupid Love? It's an adorable comedy about a couple going through a divorce. There's a scene in the movie where Steve Carell goes into his office and he's very down. No one in the office knows why. When he finally tells his boss that his wife left him, the boss starts laughing and says, "Oh, thank God. We all thought it was cancer. What a relief!"

Another benefit to being with someone who makes you laugh is, if the two of you have an argument, humor is oftentimes the best way out of it. Because, if you think about it, aren't so many arguments pretty meaningless? Laughter is the best cure for a disagreement. It's funny, there are a lot of little things about Tom that remind me of my dad, including his ability to make me laugh.

7. We respect each other.

Respect in a relationship means respecting:

1. The person's professional life (including stay-at-home parents).
2. His or her parenting style.
3. The way he or she takes care of him or herself, from the way they dress to the way they eat, exercise, stay healthy, and more.
4. The way you treat each other.
5. How he or she spends money.
6. How the person communicates, including handling conflict.
7. How he or she spends their free time.
8. His or her relationships with their family and friends.

I could go on and on. While you don't have to have immense respect for everything on this list, I will say this about respect: the more respect you have for your partner, the happier you will be in the relationship.

Why is respect so important in a relationship?

- Respect makes you feel like you are with your best friend.

  One of the wonderful things about a close friend is that you can ask your friend for advice. About anything. It can be work related, or maybe you want to ask him/her about a family situation. Anything. If you respect your partner, you will want to ask the person for advice because you know it's going to be sound advice. If you don't respect the person, you might not bother asking for any advice and you might go to other people outside of your relationship. So, what does that say about your relationship if you don't respect your partner enough to go to them first?

- Respect makes sex better.

  Good sex happens when you are attracted to someone, right? Physical attraction is important, especially at the beginning of a relationship, but more importantly, attraction stems from personality, thoughtfulness, the way you are treated, and so much more, including respect! I mean, how can you be attracted to someone and have good sex if you don't respect the person? You might have good sex for a little while, but without respect, it won't last.

- Respect makes you proud to be with your partner.

  Have you ever been in a relationship where you are out and you run into people you know, and you feel embarrassed by your partner? If so, this isn't healthy! When you respect your partner, you feel proud to be by his/her side, and you exude how you are feeling to others.

- Respect helps you trust your partner.

  Let's say, for example that you don't respect the way your spouse handles money. Well, then how can you trust him/her with the family's finances? You can't. Or let's say you don't respect how unmotivated he/she is. He/she comes home from work every night and sits on the couch and drinks. How can you trust he/she is a good role model for your kids? You can't. Respect bleeds into trust in this way.

- Respect results in better communication.

  I hear a lot from men and women about how their spouse disrespects them. One guy once said to me, "I wish my wife would be as nice to me as she is to the Starbucks barista." It is vital to a healthy romantic relationship to treat your spouse with respect. If you don't, things will all fall apart. Trust me. And, if you can't speak to your spouse with respect, then you might not respect that person. Here is an example: "Your mother is driving me crazy. I hate when she's here." This is clearly not treating your spouse with respect. Maybe the mother is awful, but that is irrelevant. It's his mother! A better way to say it is, "I know she's your mother, but she makes me uncomfortable. Would you maybe consider making plans with her from time to time on your own and without me?"

  Another example: "All you do is sit around the house! The kids are older. You should go back to work." Instead, try, "Finances are a little tough, and I think we could benefit by you getting a job. Is that something you would consider? Let's talk about it." See the difference?

- Respect increases self-esteem.

  When someone is respectful to you, it makes you feel so great about yourself, right? So, think about that when it comes to your spouse. Make your person feel important and cared about. Work is a big one. Asking about your spouse's job, planning a celebration for a work achievement, like a big sale he/she made or a promotion, or simply saying "I know how hard you work and I'm proud of you," is showing respect and lifting your spouse up at the same time. Even listening to your spouse vent about his or her job or sharing the person's enthusiasm in their job is a way of showing respect. On the flip side, when someone doesn't feel respected, self-esteem will suffer, and resentment will begin.

A statement I hear quite a bit from men and women considering divorce is, "I love my spouse, but I don't respect him or her." Since we know how important it is to have respect, you might try talking to your spouse. What do you think would happen if you sat your spouse down and said, "I love you, but I don't respect you." How will the person react? Can you have a productive conversation and ask the person to make changes? Or is it just too late? Maybe there's really nothing he or she can do to restore your respect. In that case, you can choose to live without it, or you can leave. It's a personal preference and so many factors weigh into a decision like that. Just remember this: you deserve to be treated with respect and if you are feeling disrespected, something must change if you want to be happy. That might mean divorce, that might mean counseling, that might mean expressing your feelings to your spouse. Just do something. Because mutual respect in a relationship is key to having a deep, meaningful connection and a happy life together.

8. Common interests and tastes in music, theatre, movies, travel, and more.

This is something that people who fall madly in love brush aside, and then they realize much later how important it is to enjoy common interests. People say, "What about opposites attract?" No way. I think that only applies to the first three months of a relationship. When the hotness fades a little bit, and the getting-to-know each other conversations begin to dwindle, what happens? Everyday life. That doesn't mean the relationship isn't good anymore. In fact, the relationship (if healthy) will get stronger and better. But let's face it. If the fancy dinners followed by wild sex were amazing, but you hate each other's taste in music, theatre, sports, Netflix shows, and politics, the relationship will suffer.

Of all my post-divorce relationships, I'd say Tom and I are on the same page more than any of the others. Here is one example of having interests and values in common: Tom and I take a few minutes every morning to sit and talk while I have coffee and he has water. It's just nice to sit with each other before the workday starts. At the end of each day, we do the same thing, either with a glass of wine or a cup of tea or nothing at all. Sometimes I surprise him with an appetizer. I think it's cute when he gets excited about it. We don't sit together at the end of every single day, but I'd say most days. We both enjoy it. We choose to do it because we want to feel connected.

We also enjoy the same kinds of music, theatre, movies, museums, travel, and other cultural activities. It helps that we are of a similar age. That doesn't mean you can't be happy in a relationship with a big age gap. Just make sure you have some things in common. The reason people get into serious relationships is because they want to enjoy spending time together. I also think it's healthy to introduce each other to new hobbies, passions, volunteer work, and people. The beauty of loving someone is learning from that person, being exposed to new experiences, and giving your time to do something you know he/she wants to do, also known as "taking one for the team." If your boyfriend loves hockey and you really don't, maybe surprise him with tickets to a Blackhawks game. If your girlfriend wants to go to one of those cooking places to learn how to make crisp roast duck or creamy leek soup or double chocolate layer cake, book a night to do it! Relationships are give and take, but wanting to do the same kinds of things makes life and love so much easier.

Travel is also very important. Growing up, I remember my parents taking lots of trips together, but I also remember my mom taking trips without my dad, and going with her friend who was a travel agent. I always had respect for the fact that my dad encouraged her to go on certain vacations he didn't want to go on. In other words, if one person is a traveler and the other isn't, I think the relationship can work, but both have to compromise a little bit. Also, having the same interests in where you are going is important. So, talk about this while you are dating. Actually, talk about a lot of your interests and passions while you are dating. Because you might be able to broaden his horizons a little bit, but you aren't going to change him. So, know what you are getting before you make it legal.

9. We cheer each other on.

I started Divorced Girl Smiling when I was still dating Derrek. His initial reaction was, "That's great, but I don't want my love life ending up on the internet." It was all about him, and he never even thought to encourage me or tell me he was proud of me. When I began dating Tom, Divorced Girl Smiling was about a year and a half old. I said to him, "You have to know going into this that I am going to write about our relationship. If you have a problem with that, let me know now." Tom's response: "Great! Want to have me on your podcast?" Tom also read one of my novels the first week we started dating.

Since then, Tom has been very enthusiastic about my business and is consistently cheering me on and telling me he's proud of me. When something good happens, he is the first person I tell. He's always excited. It means the world to me. And when a situation has come up that I'm not sure how to handle, Tom has been a very good sounding board and offers solid advice based on his experiences as a successful businessperson.

It's a problem if:

1. Your spouse doesn't support your career, passion, or dreams or your desire to go back to school or work.
2. He makes fun of you or gives the impression that he doesn't think you will be successful.
3. Your significant other doesn't want to hear about your new job or read even one chapter of a book you are writing.

People in happy, healthy romantic relationships are not only supportive of their partners, but are excited, no, ecstatic about the happiness they see your project is bringing you. They are truly your cheerleader, and they want you to be successful. Healthy partners aren't jealous. They don't feel threatened, like if you make it big you might dump them. A healthy relationship means being there for your spouse not only during the bad times, but during the good times—the big wins, the job offers, the money rolling in, and your face lighting up when you talk about what you do.

This works in reverse, too. It's your job to be there for your partner, too. If he has a really boring job, learn about it, anyhow. My ex-husband sold a product while we were married, and to this day, twenty-some years later, I can still rattle off his sales pitch! I took the time to listen and get involved and learn about what he did. That's big because it makes the person feel important, like their career has meaning, even if it doesn't mean that much to them. It motivates them to work harder, to do better. So, don't just pretend to care, find a way to care. If you really care about him, for the right reasons, it's not that hard.

I'm not going to lie and say that everything with Tom is perfect all the time. After living alone with my kids for 15 years, Tom and I moved in together a couple of years ago. I think that adjustment can be challenging for two people who lived independently for so long. If one picture frame is out of place, I get rattled. I have since learned to be a little less compulsive and care more about him than a bunch of out-of-place knick-knacks.

Blended families are no picnic, either. Sometimes one of his kids will have an issue with you and you don't even know why. Or you want to tell him how he should handle a certain situation as a parent, but it's really not your place because you're not the mom. Or maybe one of your kids did something that hurt him, and you apologize, realizing that it's your child who should be saying they are sorry. Most people who blend families have this Brady Bunch picture in their head, and although there are times that feel Brady Bunch-ish, they are rare. It's very complicated when you blend. The key is communicating. Be honest and talk things through with your spouse, even if it's uncomfortable or he might be hurt, or you might be afraid he will get upset. I guarantee, the second marriages that failed did not engage in this kind of communication. Instead, they chose to bury their feelings, hold on to resentment, possibly cheat, just check out, or run for the hills. That said, I know a lot of very happy blended families. But ask any of them and they will tell you it takes a lot of patience and the guts to have real conversations.

Despite all the things that can drive you nuts about someone, even in the healthiest of relationships, I think staying with someone comes down to a very basic concept: whether or not you are happy. I don't mean that you have to be happy every second, but happy in the relationship 97% of the time. That statistic might seem high since no relationship is perfect and no one is flawless, but at this point in my life—after being divorced and being in my fifties—I think I deserve the 97%. I think everyone does. I remember interviewing a divorce coach several years ago and she stated that she thought people should be happy 75% of the time. I vehemently disagreed because you know what that means? That means every week, you are unhappy at least two—maybe three days of the week! Ask yourself if you deserve that.

The last thing I'm going to say about Tom and why I think relationship works so well is: We didn't rush into marriage. We remain engaged with no plans for marriage, although we aren't ruling it out. I think so many people fall really hard for someone after divorce, and because they weren't expecting it, and because they never really thought they were capable of finding love again, they take it to the extreme and run and get married. Then, a year or so into it, they start to feel trapped, like things moved too fast, like they really didn't know the person as well as they thought (since I think everyone is on their best behavior for the first two years of a relationship). That's why the second marriage divorce rate is about 66%.

Anyone who is divorced will tell you that there's nothing worse than feeling stuck in a marriage, and that divorce is so painful they wouldn't wish it on anyone. Furthermore, people are often embarrassed and feel shame for getting divorced for a second time. So, they stay in the marriage unhappily. What I say is f*ck that. No one should stay in a marriage that isn't making them happy, or that is making them unhappy, causing them too much stress, or having an effect on their self-esteem and self-worth. If it's a bad situation, who cares what other people think? Your gut will tell you when it's time to leave and when you do, hold your head high. If people judge, they are clearly unaware that you love yourself way too much to stay in a toxic situation. The bottom line is, I am a big fan of second marriage, if it's the right time and the right person. You might want to ignore your heart and listen to your gut on this one. Remember, happily ever after does not equate to a second marriage, but rather happiness.

I hope that I'm with Tom for the rest of my life, but I won't guarantee it. Not because of anything other than the fact that one just never knows. I think anyone who has ever been divorced—even those happily remarried always have one eye open with a sliver of skepticism. What I mean is, a divorcee wouldn't say "We will never break up" because after going through the trauma of a divorce, and probably thinking that when we got married, we learn to say, "never say never." That doesn't diminish how much I value what I have with Tom. I'm just keeping things real. Things happen. People change. That is unavoidable. But there are two things you have control over in your post-divorce relationships: feeling gratitude and doing whatever you can to keep the relationship healthy. The biggest asset someone dating after divorce has is growth. In other words, if you've acknowledged your mistakes, forgiven yourself, gotten the help and support you need to make positive changes, and decided you have the guts to live the life you really want, you will be a phenomenal partner in a romantic relationship. And phenomenal partners end up with phenomenal people.

PART II

YOU

CHAPTER 12

The Divorced Man:
What You Need to Know

I'm not a man (obviously) but I have to say that I know the divorced man very, very well. I got divorced in 2008, and since then, I've met, talked to, interviewed, dated, and hung out in suburban bars with enough divorced men to make me somewhat of an expert on who these guys really are. I'm generalizing, of course. Not all divorced men are the same, and each person has his own, unique qualities. But here is how I feel. At his core, a divorced man is a wounded soul who in many ways has a harder time than his spouse with the divorce, though it may not appear that way. The divorced man needs sex. Badly. He wants the validation that he is still attractive to women. The divorced man wants a girlfriend—but not really. Perhaps the most prevalent characteristic of a divorced man is that he just wants to be loved. He craves having a spouse who in his words, "gives a shit about him."

Here is my take on the top 10 emotions of a man going through a divorce:

1. Shock

In my opinion, most men don't leave their wives unless they are leaving for another woman. So, if a man is the one who wanted the divorce, and he already has someone else, he usually doesn't feel shock. But, if his wife leaves him, I think so many men are utterly shocked. Even if the wife has been threatening to divorce him for years, once she pulls the trigger, there is still a sense of disbelief, leaving a man feeling like this doesn't even feel real. It can be traumatic.

2. Fear

In most divorce scenarios, it's the husband who moves out of the house. I can't count the number of men I met after my divorce who were living in small apartments and having their kids every Wednesday night and every other weekend. And most of them were very sensitive when it came to talking about spending time with their kids. They wanted me to know they saw their kids on a regular basis, almost as if they were insecure about it and had to prove to the world they were still a good father. Of course they are still good fathers!

I feel so sad when I think about how it must feel to have to move out of your home, especially if you aren't the one who wanted the divorce, and then try to work 40-50 hours a week, and then find time to care for the kids, oftentimes having to learn for the first time how to cook, clean, and do things like Mom does. Also, think about how much anxiety a guy might feel, wondering if their kids are going to be closer to Mom because they spend more time with her, and how much pressure that puts on him. I'm not saying women don't feel these feelings too. They absolutely do.

3. Resentment

Resentment is almost always present. Almost everyone getting divorced feels resentment towards their spouse, which might go back months and years. The divorced man might be thinking: "I was a good husband. I didn't cheat. I always provided for the family. I'm a good dad... and she never appreciated me. She was mean to me, and she never wanted to have sex with me..." These thoughts breed resentment and with resentment comes anger.

4. Anger

In divorce, there's a lot to be angry about and a lot of people to be angry with. A man might be angry with the situation. He might be angry with his wife for divorcing him. He might be thinking: "Why would she do this? We have such a great life!" He might be angry with her for doing this to the kids. He might be angry with God. He might be angry at the world. He might be angry with all women. And perhaps the biggest: he might be angry at the justice system because he has to give her money or he didn't get the visitation schedule he wanted.

I find that men of all income brackets, from the super wealthy to the financially struggling, cannot stand giving their ex child support and/or alimony. It doesn't matter who left who. Many men truly resent handing over that check every month. It kills them, even if money is no issue. It also makes them angry and causes so much conflict in a divorce.

5. Rejection

Men getting divorced feel, to me, like they are wounded. They have been hurt, and because they are men, they often feel as if they can't really show their hurt and vulnerability. They feel like they have to be strong. They might also feel rejected: she doesn't want me anymore. She's beaten me down for so long and made me feel bad about myself for so long so maybe what she thinks about me is right.

The insecurity of feeling wounded and rejected often shows up in dating. Some men want to get married again as quickly as possible, desperate to find someone again, while others become commitment-phobic, running from serious relationships and only wanting a casual fling. Some men don't even know what they want. They think they want one thing and behave as if they want another.

6. Physical Insecurity

I feel like a lot of men seek out sex after divorce as a way to prove to themselves that they are still desirable to women. They need to feel validated: "I'm still attractive to other women, I can still perform well, I'm still young, and these women appreciate sex with me so much more than my ex ever did!"

7. Financial Anxiety

Men not only resent having to pay their ex child support or alimony, but they might become worried about their finances. What they used to save after a paycheck is oftentimes cut in half and that's a hard pill to swallow! Plus, now they have another residence, whether they bought a new home or they rent. I truly think financial anxiety is one of the most stressful aspects of a divorce for men. With fear and anxiety comes resentment and anger towards the ex, since in their mind, they feel like, "Why is she doing this? Things were so much easier when we were together."

8. Sadness

Men going through divorce also feel sadness. They feel sad for themselves, but also sad for the kids. They might feel like a failure and feel shame or embarrassment about the divorce. These feelings can cause sadness, too. Plus, a man might still love his ex-wife. He might have regrets about the way he treated her or the way he handled things or didn't handle things by not trying therapy when she wanted it. So often, I see women try for years to save the marriage, and when they finally give up, men want to work on it. It's so sad, and I feel for both partners. Sadness can often turn to feelings of regret, as well. Men have told me, "I wish I could turn the clock back. I'd do so many things differently."

9. Jealousy

I've seen this scenario so much: the wife starts dating someone and the ex has a really hard time with it. They might say to their ex, "How do you know it's safe to have this guy around our kids?" They might have a point, but oftentimes, it's more of a jealousy and territorial thing. The last thing they want is for the kids to become close with another man, but they might also be unable to handle picturing their wife with someone else. I see this even if it was the man who wanted the divorce. On a side note, women have these same feelings—sometimes worse! I am guilty of it and have heard from countless women that their ex getting a girlfriend infuriates them.

10. Surprise

Countless divorced men have told me how shocked they were at all the attention and opportunities for relationships and sex they have from single women. It usually goes something like this: A man gets divorced and has no idea how attractive he is to other women. All of a sudden, everyone and their brother wants to set him up. Women are all over him and he cannot believe it. Suddenly he gets a little bit cocky.

These stories make me happy because they help men realize that they have a self-esteem problem, and oftentimes it causes them to dig deeper (meaning go to therapy). Having a girlfriend (or dating a lot) also keeps the divorced man cheerful, and he might be a little nicer to his ex. Again, although every divorce story is unique, I have known all kinds of divorced men who display some or all of these 10 feelings. Having these feelings doesn't make a man a bad person, a bad father, a weak person, or even someone who is unworthy of finding a great partner. I feel for men going through a divorce. I understand their anxieties and fears, and I admire so many of their wonderful qualities, especially when it comes to being a single dad.

CHAPTER 13

Are You Ready for Love?

"**I** can't meet anyone."
"There are no good guys out there."
"I'm going to be alone forever."

I hear women say this of often when it comes to dating after divorce over the age of 40. I'm not going to disagree and say it's easy to meet Mr. Right. It took me 49 years! But what I will say is that timing plays a huge role in finding love, and if you aren't emotionally ready for the love of your life, timing doesn't matter because it will not happen, no matter how many dates you have.

You could be walking down the street and pass the greatest guy on earth, but if you aren't in the right frame of mind, you won't even notice him. Maybe you're not happy with yourself. Maybe you still aren't over your last boyfriend or your ex-husband. Maybe you're tired of living where you live, and you feel like you need to move. Maybe you haven't truly worked out the issues you have that are preventing you from being in a healthy relationship. Or maybe you haven't figured out yet that dating womanizers just doesn't work. The chances of meeting someone significant in any of these circumstances is minimal.

Can you control whether or not you find love? Yes and no. There are two things you can't control: fate and other people. The one person you can control is you. You can control:

Your physical appearance.

I'm not saying you have to lose weight or undergo plastic surgery to find a boyfriend, but rather if you are happy with the way you look and feel, you are more likely to walk into a date poised, confident, and radiant. Have you ever considered going out on a date without makeup? Probably not. So, maybe all you need to feel more self-confident is an after-divorce makeover. That could mean new makeup or some new outfits or some skin treatments. Look, say what you will, but there's a reason Botox is a billion-dollar industry. This all might sound very superficial, so I want to make it clear that you don't have to do any of it. But what you do have to do is walk out the door for every date feeling confident about the way you look. You owe that to yourself. That feeling means something unique to every person. So, whatever it is that is going to make you feel like a million bucks, do it!

Your attitude in dating.

I understand. The dating apps are a nightmare. You are so tired of having conversations with people who end up ghosting you. Rejection (even though it's not personal, in my opinion) can feel exhausting, and meeting loser after loser after loser can feel hopeless. The key is patience. Remember, you only need one! If you feel burned out and need to take a break from time to time, do it. Don't put a timeline on finding love and don't put pressure on yourself. This kind of attitude will help minimize disappointment and frustration and will turn dating from a chore into an adventure.

The quality of men you choose to date.

If you have a pattern of dating men who drink a lot or who are married or who are abusive, you are setting yourself up to stay single. Recognizing negative patterns and men who aren't a good fit for you is key in changing the outcome of your relationship success. Keep telling yourself, "I deserve better."

How you act/present yourself on a date.

Dating behavior, particularly on dates one and two, is pretty simple. Smile a lot, be a good listener, and keep things light. Ask a lot of questions. Remember, you are interviewing him. A lot of women will say to themselves before going on a date, "I hope he likes me." Well guess what? How about changing that sentence to, "I hope I like him!" Also, try to have fun. I know you're nervous and you're so tired of being disappointed, but if you don't expect too much—in fact just expect to meet someone nice and interesting—you might walk away feeling gratitude instead of feeling let down. No date is ever a waste. Something good can come from every date. It's all in shifting your mindset to looking for that good thing. A guy who isn't your dream guy might become the friend who introduces you to your dream guy. He might share a good book or a hobby or a great restaurant with you. And he might just be a really really nice guy who would be a great boyfriend to someone else you know. Be yourself on every date and always be kind no matter what. You have no idea what this other person is going through.

Thinking about your ex.

If you aren't over your ex, you have zero chance of being in a healthy, happy romantic relationship. Have you ever talked to someone years after their divorce, and they are still constantly talking about what a jerk their ex is? This is the kind of person no one wants to be around. Some people are still in love with their ex and can't let go. Others are simply obsessed. If you are still harboring anger and resentment or love or hate, I'm not telling you to let it go because I know it's not that simple. I get it. My advice is to get help so that you can let it go. Help means a therapist or a divorce coach or a self-help book or a spiritual advisor or a retreat or a support group. I promise you, if you work on yourself, you will feel better and you will present so much better on dates. People love people who are positive and happy, but that has to be genuine, and people can see through it if it isn't.

Self-love.

I want to say something I feel so incredibly passionate about: The best kind of love you can ever have in your life is self-love. If you have self-love, you won't be a lonely person and you won't feel alone. People who have self-love don't feel desperate to have a spouse, and they are comfortable being single. It makes sense, doesn't it? If you love yourself, then you want to spend time with yourself, right? Also, if you have self-love, you will be in a better mood so much more often, and you will be more successful, both professionally and in your personal relationships, because deep down, you will have more self-worth.

How do you get and keep self-love? By giving yourself a break. By forgiving yourself for your past mistakes or for how you might have acted during parts of your marriage. You also obtain self-love by applauding and rewarding yourself when you do something really great. If you get a raise at work and there's something you really want to buy, if you love yourself, you should buy it. If you're proud of yourself, look in the mirror and acknowledge that you're proud of yourself! You also get and keep self-love by treating others with respect and by giving those you love and the rest of the world the best you have to offer. When you go to bed at night, ask yourself, "How did I spend my day? Did I make anyone else's day better? Did I do something nice for someone or for myself? Self-love can also start by making changes. The changes can be basic, such as nurturing your body with better food, physical exercise, and more self-care, or they can be more complex, like starting a new career, having the guts to really go to therapy this time and commit long-term—not just once or twice, engaging in volunteer work, or calling up an old friend to make amends, even if it's been a decade. The more you like yourself, the better chance you have of finding love. You know why? Because when you feel like you deserve to be loved, there's so much less insecurity and so much more vulnerability in the relationship.

Health and Wellness, and How They Tie into Good Love

We are constantly being told by our doctors to eat healthy, exercise, and maintain a sensible weight for the purpose of living a longer, better quality of life. But what doctors don't really get into is how doing those things can benefit or hurt your romantic relationships. Being fit and healthy leads to countless pluses, including: more energy, a better emotional outlook, a sharper mind, more success at work, more productivity, and more confidence. All of these things and other wellness benefits roll over into our love lives.

For example, let's say you've put on 15 pounds as you've gotten older and you're unhappy about it. So, you decide to join Orange Theory Fitness, and you commit to two classes per week for 4 weeks. You then decide to stop drinking alcohol, and you stick to an eating regime of 1500 calories per day. Within two months, you've lost 10 pounds. Now, you feel proud of yourself, not to mention all the other health benefits you are experiencing. But something else happens. You start to feel sexy and pretty, and that comes across to your dates, who, by the way, probably never would have thought you needed to lose those 15 pounds. The biggest difference isn't the weight; it's your newfound self-confidence, the way you present, and your happiness.

Health and wellness can also impact relationships negatively. Let's say a spouse is diagnosed with diabetes, and the doctor recommends changing his or her diet and exercise to lower blood sugar and better manage the condition. But the spouse doesn't have the discipline or desire to comply. This can be frustrating to their partner and can also cause anger and resentment. As couples age together, it's important not just to take care of each other, but to be responsible and disciplined when it comes to your own health. The bottom line is, when couples are physically healthier, they are happier.

If you like the book, you'll love the Divorced Girl Smiling website!

CHAPTER 14

The Power of Hope

I'm not sure there are many things in life that are worse than the feeling of loneliness. As humans, it's in our nature to need love and intimacy to thrive. If we don't have food, we will die. If we don't have water, we will die. If we don't have love? I'm not sure we will physically die, but it can cause unbearable pain and suffering that can have a negative effect on our emotional and physical health.

There is one thing that throughout my life has kept me sane and motivated not to give up on love. That one thing is hope. Hope means that you never give up on your desire to find love, and that in your mind, you know at some point you will. You just know it. Sure, there have been times in my life that hope left me for a little while, and I would be in tears, thinking, "What if I never find love again?" Remember the day I was walking down Clark Street? The day I met my now ex-husband? It felt unfair and it made me angry and sad and depressed. But hope has a way of inching back into the soul if you have faith in God, in others, and of course, in yourself.

I truly believe in fate, but I also think we help guide fate depending on our actions. For example, the chances of meeting someone significant are zero if you are sitting on your couch watching TV. But if you agree to meet your friend at a coffee shop or a bar, your chances of meeting someone immediately increase. You could meet a cute guy who happens to be sitting at the next table. Even going to a gas station theoretically increases your chances of finding love. Every morning, if you are blessed to be waking up, you never know what can happen and who you could meet. This applies to dating apps, as well. If you decide to close your Bumble account, you won't meet a man that way. If you continue to swipe right and left, even if it's just a few minutes a day, at least there's a chance. There are times we all need a break from dating and trying to find love, and that's perfectly fine. Just don't give up permanently.

There's a fine line between not making any effort and just waiting for love to come to you, versus trying too hard by putting pressure on yourself and dating and dating and dating like it's a chore. Somewhere in the middle is good and maintaining hope at all times is even better. Hope means that you keep living your authentic happy life, doing what you love, surrounding yourself with people who make you happy, and distancing yourself from toxicity. Know that he's out there, and that three things will lead you to him: self-love, faith, and of course, hope.

CONCLUSION

The Importance of Dating Dogs

One of the most valuable things I hope you to take away from this book is this: From every bad date, every tear you shed over some guy, every relationship that ends leaving you weary, and every time you feel like there are no good men out there, something happens: You learn something, and these lessons can be gems. Here's a snapshot of what I learned, just from the dogs in this book (there were other dogs, believe me.):

1. The Bichon Frise (Mike, the one-night stand guy): No one is perfect, and we all do things that feel wrong and shameful. Learn how to forgive yourself and not feel guilty.

2. The German Shepherd (Brad, the hot and cold guy), The Golden Retriever (Noah, the way too nice guy), and The Rottweiler (Drew, the addict): You deserve to be treated wonderfully. If someone is treating you in a way that doesn't feel right and/or doesn't make you happy, you owe it to yourself to leave. Appreciate and recognize the ones who treat you well and treat them just as good!

3. The Maltese (Jeff, the Vince Vaughn Lookalike): You don't need a man to validate that you are sexy and desirable. You are. Period.

4. The Jack Russell Terrier (Derrek, the cheater): If you suspect he is cheating, you're not paranoid, you're right. Also, you deserve to be

with someone who wants to be with just you. I have a no-tolerance policy for cheating, lying and gaslighting.

5. The Beagle (Scott, My Mr. Big): If you really want someone in your life, you are doing yourself a favor by accepting what they are willing to give. So, if he just wants to be friends you have two choices: never see him again or be his friend, which I think you will benefit from.

6. The Dalmatian (Chris, the Denzel Washington Lookalike): Timing is everything and something that is out of your control.

7. The Labradoodle (Veronica, the lesbian): Being honest and upfront in relationships will foster self-love and will bring good karma back to you.

8. The Goldendoodle (Tom, the hot baseball coach): We show up differently in each and every relationship we are in. If he brings out the best in you, that's a huge indication he's the one.

What have you learned from your dogs? Instead of looking at them as a waste of my time, a loser, a psycho, a liar, a cheater, or an annoyance, try to think of your dogs as gifts. They're giving you life experience, wisdom, and perhaps a few laughs, and they are helping you learn about yourself—about what you want and what you feel you deserve when it comes to love. So, when you come home from a date and you think, "Thank God that's over," instead, say to yourself, "Good boy!" He's showed you more of what you don't want, so that when that perfect breed comes along, you'll be able to recognize him, appreciate him, and never, ever let him go.

People have such a love-hate relationship with dating, because truly, dating can feel like a roller coaster. One day you think you might have met your husband, the next, he tells you he's ending it and your hopes come crashing down. A promising relationship can feel incredibly electrifying, but the shoe can drop at any minute. That roller coaster ride can feel exhausting. I get it. But one day, you'll meet someone and the shoe won't drop. He won't break up with you. And then you'll find yourself in love, and maybe even walking down the aisle again if that's what you want. Remember these four words: You only need one. That's it. One. When you find that person, the one, you might find yourself smiling from time to time at the thought of all your dogs. After all, as difficult as each one was, and as much heartache as they caused you, each of those furry friends will have led you to where you are right now and who you are with at this moment, and you'll be filled with gratitude, peace, and real, authentic love. And you might realize that you are forever grateful for the gift of this journey you took with them. I know I am.

From the bottom of my heart, I wish you all the best in your dating after divorce journey, and I hope you find love that brings you more joy than you ever thought possible.
Love, Jackie

ACKNOWLEDGMENTS

I was sitting on the balcony of my parents' home in 2013 when my dad and I started talking about combining my divorce experience and my love of writing. He convinced me to start a blog, which would turn into my business, mission and passion: Divorced Girl Smiling. So, he is the first person I'd like to thank. Not only did my dad come up with the idea, but for years, he coached me and rooted for me and was a huge influence in my business. Watching him run his successful company when I was in junior high school, high school, and college had a big impact on me and gave me the entrepreneurial spirit, courage, drive and determination to run my own business. Even now, he's gone, but I still feel his spirit and advice so often. Thank you, Dad. I also want to thank my mom for her support, friendship, and love. Thank you, Mom, for all your great suggestions, and for never saying "I told you so," even though you could have about 10,000 times.

Thank you, John, the love of my life, (Hot Baseball Coach) for your love, encouragement and support. I never could have written this book without the understanding of true love, which I wouldn't have experienced without you. Thank you to my kids, Isaac and Anna, two more loves of my life, (and my dog, Jackson, too!) and thank you to my family, including John's kids. You guys are the best and not a day goes by that I don't feel immense gratitude for each of you.

I want to thank all my Divorced Girl Smiling trusted professionals. I am deeply impressed by the hard work, dedication, and enthusiasm you have for your careers. Working with people going through a divorce day after day after day and for years, isn't easy. Hearing sad stories, watching people fall apart, and being alongside for their anger, frustration and fear can be exhausting. I have so much respect for your passion and commitment and I'm grateful for your partnerships. I'm so proud to know you.

To the Divorced Girl Smiling community—all the people who read the DGS articles, listen to the DGS podcast, follow us on social media, and reach out to the DGS trusted professionals, you are the reason I jump out of bed every morning to start working. Thank you for your emails: the ones thanking me, the ones telling me you didn't like something I wrote or said, and the ones you wrote seeking advice at 2:00 a.m. because you couldn't sleep and didn't know who else to turn to. It means the world that you trust me. To see so many of you go from devastated and scared to empowered and happy (and many in love) is beyond fulfilling and gives my life purpose.

Thank you to my friends, mentors and people who have supported me: Mark Cuban for believing and investing in Divorced Girl Smiling, Dan Stefani, Elaine Moss, Pete Mullins, Jason Price, Anna Krolikowska, Tiffany Hughes, Katherine Miller, Brian James, Ellen Feldman, Phil LaGiglia, Michael Cohen, Rob Elder, Margalit Tocher, Jordan Feiger, Norberto Kogan, Loryn Kogan, the late Jennifer Devine, Alisa Bay, Paige Morrow Kimball, Paula Giovacchini, Ann Adelman, Justin Scheef, Rob Floyd, Julia Pastore, Jill Lawlor, and Mindy Garfinkle.

I'd like to thank all of the real people on whom I based my dogs and stories. Thanks for the material! But honestly, I hope reading the book didn't hurt you or cause you to think I don't care about you because I do. But this book was about me and my life, and the stories are told from my perspective. They were written not out of spite, but as a way for me to entertain, inspire and help people in dating after divorce. Thank you for understanding.

Lastly, to anyone who is looking for true love, please don't lose hope or give up. You are beautiful and you deserve to find it. But remember that the most important love of all is self-love. Be kind to yourself and always remember that every time you smile, you get prettier.

ABOUT THE AUTHOR

Jackie Pilossoph is Founder of DIVORCED GIRL SMILING, the company that connects people facing divorce with trusted, vetted divorce professionals. Divorced Girl Smiling (DGS) is also a podcast, website, mobile app, and well-known brand and community. DGS has a mission to empower, connect and inspire men and women before, during and after divorce. Pilossoph, who holds a master's degree in Broadcast Journalism, is a former television news reporter, as well as a former features reporter and writer for the Chicago Tribune. Her syndicated weekly column, LOVE ESSENTIALLY, was published in The Pioneer Press, The Chicago Tribune, and all Tribune Publishing editions, as well as Better Magazine. Pilossoph was also a Huffington Post divorce blogger for five years. Oh, and she went through a divorce (obviously.) To learn more, visit: www.divorcedgirlsmiling.com. Email Jackie: Jackie@divorcedgirlsmiling.com.

Visit
DivorcedGirlSmiling.com

Listen to the Divorced Girl
Smiling Podcast

www.ingramcontent.com/pod-product-compliance
Lightning Source LLC
Chambersburg PA
CBHW020350130626
46549CB00006B/2249